# STATUTORY SUPPLEMENT TO CASES AND MATERIALS ON

# LABOR LAW

## COLLECTIVE BARGAINING IN A FREE SOCIETY

### Third Edition

By

**Walter E. Oberer**
*Professor of Law*
*University of Utah*

**Kurt L. Hanslowe**
*Late Professor of Law and*
*Professor of Industrial and Labor Relations*
*Cornell University*

**Jerry R. Andersen**
*Late Professor of Law*
*University of Utah*

**Timothy J. Heinsz**
*Professor of Law*
*University of Missouri-Columbia*

**AMERICAN CASEBOOK SERIES**

**WEST PUBLISHING CO.**
ST. PAUL, MINN., 1986

# TABLE OF CONTENTS

———

*

# Statutory Supplement

## to

## CASES AND MATERIALS

### ON

# LABOR LAW

## SHERMAN ANTITRUST ACT

26 Stat. 209 (1890), as amended, 15 U.S.C. §§ 1–7 (1982).

**Sec. 1.** Every contract, combination in the form of trust or otherwise, or conspiracy, in restraint of trade or commerce among the several States, or with foreign nations, is hereby declared to be illegal. Every person who shall make any contract or engage in any combination or conspiracy hereby declared to be illegal shall be deemed guilty of a felony, and, on conviction thereof, shall be punished by fine not exceeding one million dollars if a corporation, or, if any other person, one hundred thousand dollars, or by imprisonment not exceeding three years, or by both said punishments, in the discretion of the court.

**Sec. 2.** Every person who shall monopolize, or attempt to monopolize, or combine or conspire with any other person or persons, to monopolize any part of the trade or commerce among the several States, or with foreign nations, shall be deemed guilty of a felony, and, on conviction thereof, shall be punished by fine not exceeding one million dollars if a corporation, or, if any other person, one hundred thousand dollars, or by imprisonment not exceeding three years, or by both said punishments, in the discretion of the court.*

\* \* \*

**Sec. 4.** The several district courts of the United States are invested with jurisdiction to prevent and restrain violations of this act; and it shall be the duty of the several United States attorneys, in their respective districts, under the direction of the Attorney General, to institute proceedings in equity to prevent and restrain such violations. Such proceedings may be by way of petition setting forth the case and praying that such violation shall be enjoined or otherwise prohibited.

* Prior to 1974 violations of the Sherman Act were misdemeanors carrying penalties of fines up to $50,000 and of prison terms of up to one year. The increased penalties were provided for in Pub.L. No. 93–528, 83, 88 Stat. 1708, Dec. 21, 1974.

When the parties complained of shall have been duly notified of such petition the court shall proceed, as soon as may be, to the hearing and determination of the case; and pending such petition and before final decree, the court may at any time make such temporary restraining order or prohibition as shall be deemed just in the premises.

**Sec. 5.** Whenever it shall appear to the court before which any proceeding under section 4 of this act may be pending, that the ends of justice require that other parties should be brought before the court, the court may cause them to be summoned, whether they reside in the district in which the court is held or not; and subpoenas to that end may be served in any district by the marshal thereof.

**Sec. 6.** Any property owned under any contract or by any combination, or pursuant to any conspiracy (and being the subject thereof) mentioned in section 1 of this act, and being in the course of transportation from one State to another, or to a foreign country, shall be forfeited to the United States, and may be seized and condemned by like proceedings as those provided by law for the forfeiture, seizure, and condemnation of property imported into the United States contrary to law.

**Sec. 7.** Any person who shall be injured in his business or property by any other person or corporation by reason of anything forbidden or declared to be unlawful by this act, may sue therefor in any circuit court of the United States in the district in which the defendant resides or is found, without respect to the amount in controversy, and shall recover threefold the damage by him sustained, and the costs of suit, including a reasonable attorney's fee.*

**Sec. 8.** The word "person," or "persons," wherever used in this act shall be deemed to include corporations and associations existing under or authorized by the laws of either the United States, the laws of any of the Territories, the laws of any State, or the laws of any foreign country.

---

\* Section 7 was repealed by 69 Stat. 283 (1955), without, however, adversely affecting the remedies available for antitrust violations since Section 4 of the Clayton Antitrust Act of 1914, infra, independently authorizes suits for treble damages. A new Section 7 was inserted by Section 402 of the "Foreign Trade Antitrust Improvements Act of 1982," 96 Stat. 1246:

"This Act shall not apply to conduct involving trade or commerce (other than import trade or import commerce) with foreign nations unless—

"(1) such conduct has a direct, substantial, and reasonably foreseeable effect—

"(A) on trade or commerce which is not trade or commerce with foreign nations, or on import trade or import commerce with foreign nations; or

"(B) on export trade or export commerce with foreign nations, of a person engaged in such trade or commerce in the United States; and

"(2) such effect gives rise to a claim under the provisions of this Act, other than this section.

"If this Act applies to such conduct only because of the operation of paragraph (1)(B), then this Act shall apply to such conduct only for injury to export business in the United States."

# CLAYTON ANTITRUST ACT

38 Stat. 730 (1914), as amended, 15 U.S.C. §§ 15, 17, 26 (1982),
29 U.S.C. § 52 (1982).

*Be it enacted by the Senate and House of Representatives of the United States of America in Congress Assembled,* That "antitrust laws," as used herein, includes the Act entitled "An Act to protect trade and commerce against unlawful restraints and monopolies," approved July second, eighteen hundred and ninety [Sherman Act] * * *.

**Sec. 4.** * * * [That] any person who shall be injured in his business or property by reason of anything forbidden in the antitrust laws may sue therefor in any district court of the United States in the district in which the defendant resides or is found or has an agent, without respect to the amount in controversy, and shall recover threefold the damages by him sustained, and the cost of suit, including a reasonable attorney's fee.

**Sec. 6.** That the labor of a human being is not a commodity or article of commerce. Nothing contained in the antitrust laws shall be construed to forbid the existence and operation of labor, agricultural, or horticultural organizations, instituted for the purposes of mutual help, and not having capital stock or conducted for profit, or to forbid or restrain individual members of such organizations from lawfully carrying out the legitimate objects thereof; nor shall such organizations, or the members thereof, be held or construed to be illegal combinations or conspiracies in restraint of trade, under the antitrust laws.

**Sec. 16.** That any person, firm, corporation, or association shall be entitled to sue for and have injunctive relief, in any court of the United States having jurisdiction over the parties, against threatened loss or damage by a violation of the antitrust laws, including sections 2, 3, 7, and 8 of this Act, when and under the same conditions and principles as injunctive relief against threatened conduct that will cause loss or damage is granted by courts of equity, under the rules governing such proceedings, and upon the execution of proper bond against damages for an injunction improvidently granted and a showing that the danger of irreparable loss or damage is immediate, a preliminary injunction may issue: *Provided,* That nothing herein contained shall be construed to entitle any person, firm, corporation, or association, except the United States, to bring suit in equity for injunctive relief against any common carrier subject to the provisions of the Act to regulate commerce, approved February fourth, eighteen hundred and eighty-seven, in respect of any matter subject to the regulation, supervision, or other jurisdiction of the Interstate Commerce Commission. In any action under this section in which the plaintiff substantially prevails, the court shall award the cost of suit, including a reasonable attorney's fee, to such plaintiff.*

**Sec. 20.** That no restraining order or injunction shall be granted by any court of the United States, or a judge or the judges thereof, in any case between an employer and employees, or between employers and employees, or between employees, or between persons employed and persons seeking employment, involving, or growing out of, a dispute concerning terms or conditions of employment, unless necessary to prevent irreparable injury to property, or to a property right, of the party making the application, for which injury there is no adequate remedy at law, and such property or property right must be described with particularity in the application, which must be in writing and sworn to by the applicant or by his agent or attorney.

And no such restraining order or injunction shall prohibit any person or persons, whether singly or in concert, from terminating any relation of employment, or from ceasing to perform any work or labor, or from recommending, advising, or persuading others by peaceful means so to do; or from attending at any place where any such person or persons may lawfully be, for the purpose of peacefully obtaining or communicating information, or from peacefully persuading any person to work or to abstain from working; or from ceasing to patronize or to employ any party to such dispute, or from recommending, advising, or persuading others by peaceful and lawful means so to do; or from paying or giving to, or withholding from, any person engaged in such dispute, any strike benefits or other moneys or things of value; or from peaceably assembling in a lawful manner, and for lawful purposes; or from doing any act or thing which might lawfully be done in the absence of such dispute by any party thereto; nor shall any of the acts specified in this paragraph be considered or held to be violations of any law of the United States.

* The last sentence was added to Section 16 by Pub.L. No. 94–435, Title III, § 302(3), 90 Stat. 1396, Sept. 30, 1976.

# NORRIS–LAGUARDIA ACT

47 Stat. 70 (1932), as amended 29 U.S.C. §§ 101–15 (1982).

### AN ACT

To amend the Judicial Code and to define and limit the jurisdiction of courts sitting in equity, and for other purposes.

### Sec. 1.  Issuance of restraining orders and injunctions; limitation; public policy.

No court of the United States, as herein defined, shall have jurisdiction to issue any restraining order or temporary or permanent injunction in a case involving or growing out of a labor dispute, except in a strict conformity with the provisions of this Act; nor shall any such restraining order or temporary or permanent injunction be issued contrary to the public policy declared in this Act.

### Sec. 2.  Public policy in labor matters declared.

In the interpretation of this Act and in determining the jurisdiction and authority of the courts of the United States, as such jurisdiction and authority are herein defined and limited, the public policy of the United States is hereby declared as follows:

Whereas under prevailing economic conditions, developed with the aid of governmental authority for owners of property to organize in the corporate and other forms of ownership association, the individual unorganized worker is commonly helpless to exercise actual liberty of contract and to protect his freedom of labor, and thereby to obtain acceptable terms and conditions of employment, wherefore, though he should be free to decline to associate with his fellows, it is necessary that he have full freedom of association, self-organization, and designation of representatives of his own choosing, to negotiate the terms and conditions of his employment, and that he shall be free from the interference, restraint, or coercion of employers of labor, or their agents, in the designation of such representatives or in self-organization or in other concerted activities for the purpose of collective bargaining or other mutual aid or protection; therefore, the following definitions of and limitations upon the jurisdiction and authority of the courts of the United States are enacted.

### Sec. 3.  Nonenforceability of undertakings in conflict with public policy; "yellow dog" contracts.

Any undertaking or promise, such as is described in this section, or any other undertaking or promise in conflict with the public policy declared in section 2 of this Act is hereby declared to be contrary to the public policy of the United States, shall not be enforceable in any court of the United States and shall not afford any basis for the granting of legal or equitable relief by any such court, including specifically the following:

Every undertaking or promise hereafter made, whether written or oral, express or implied, constituting or contained in any contract or agreement of hiring or employment between any individual, firm, company, association, or corporation, and any employee or prospective employee of the same, whereby

(a) Either party to such contract or agreement undertakes or promises not to join, become, or remain a member of any labor organization or of any employer organization; or

(b) Either party to such contract or agreement undertakes or promises that he will withdraw from an employment relation in the event that he joins, becomes, or remains a member of any labor organization or of any employer organization.

### Sec. 4. Enumeration of specific acts not subject to restraining orders or injunctions.

No court of the United States shall have jurisdiction to issue any restraining order or temporary or permanent injunction in any case involving or growing out of any labor dispute to prohibit any person or persons participating or interested in such dispute (as these terms are herein defined) from doing, whether singly or in concert, any of the following acts:

(a) Ceasing or refusing to perform any work or to remain in any relation of employment;

(b) Becoming or remaining a member of any labor organization or of any employer organization, regardless of any such undertaking or promise as is described in section 3 of this Act;

(c) Paying or giving to, or withholding from, any person participating or interested in such labor dispute, any strike or unemployment benefits or insurance, or other moneys or things of value;

(d) By all lawful means aiding any person participating or interested in any labor dispute who is being proceeded against in, or is prosecuting, any action or suit in any court of the United States or of any State;

(e) Giving publicity to the existence of, or the facts involved in, any labor dispute, whether by advertising, speaking, patrolling, or by any other method not involving fraud or violence;

(f) Assembling peaceably to act or to organize to act in promotion of their interests in a labor dispute;

(g) Advising or notifying any person of an intention to do any of the acts heretofore specified;

(h) Agreeing with other persons to do or not to do any of the acts heretofore specified; and

(i) Advising, urging, or otherwise causing or inducing without fraud or violence the acts heretofore specified, regardless of any such undertaking or promise as is described in section 3 of this Act.

### Sec. 5. Doing in concert of certain acts as constituting unlawful combination or conspiracy subjecting person to injunctive remedies.

No court of the United States shall have jurisdiction to issue a restraining order or temporary or permanent injunction upon the ground that any of the persons participating or interested in a labor dispute constitute or are engaged in an unlawful combination or conspiracy because of the doing in concert of the acts enumerated in section 4 of this Act.

### Sec. 6. Responsibility of officers and members of associations or their organizations for unlawful acts of individual officers, members, and agents.

No officer or member of any association or organization, and no association or organization participating or interested in a labor dispute, shall be held responsible or liable in any court of the United States for the unlawful acts of individual officers, members, or agents, except upon clear proof of actual participation in, or actual authorization of, such acts, or of ratification of such acts after actual knowledge thereof.

### Sec. 7. Issuance of injunctions in labor disputes; hearings; findings of court; notice to affected persons; temporary restraining order; undertakings.

No court of the United States shall have jurisdiction to issue a temporary or permanent injunction in any case involving or growing out of a labor dispute, as herein defined, except after hearing the testimony of witnesses in open court (with opportunity for cross-examination) in support of the allegations of a complaint made under oath, and testimony in opposition thereto, if offered, and except after findings of fact by the court, to the effect—

(a) That unlawful acts have been threatened and will be committed unless restrained or have been committed and will be continued unless restrained, but no injunction or temporary restraining order shall be issued on account of any threat or unlawful act excepting against the person or persons, association, or organization making the threat or committing the unlawful act or actually authorizing or ratifying the same after actual knowledge thereof;

(b) That substantial and irreparable injury to complainant's property will follow;

(c) That as to each item of relief granted greater injury will be inflicted upon complainant by the denial of relief than will be inflicted upon defendants by the granting of relief;

(d) That complainant has no adequate remedy at law; and

(e) That the public officers charged with the duty to protect complainant's property are unable or unwilling to furnish adequate protection.

Such hearing shall be held after due and personal notice thereof has been given, in such manner as the court shall direct, to all known persons against whom relief is sought, and also to the chief of those public officials of the county and city within which the unlawful acts have been threatened or committed charged with the duty to protect complainant's property: *Provided, however,* That if a complainant shall also allege that, unless a temporary restraining order shall be issued without notice, a substantial and irreparable injury to complainant's property will be unavoidable, such a temporary restraining order may be issued upon testimony under oath, sufficient, if sustained, to justify the court in issuing a temporary injunction upon a hearing after notice. Such a temporary restraining order shall be effective for no longer than five days and shall become void at the expiration of said five days. No temporary restraining order or temporary injunction shall be issued except on condition that complainant shall first file an undertaking with adequate security in an amount to be fixed by the court sufficient to recompense those enjoined for any loss, expense, or damage caused by the improvident or erroneous issuance of such order or injunction, including all reasonable costs (together with a reasonable attorney's fee) and expense of defense against the order or against the granting of any injunctive relief sought in the same proceeding and subsequently denied by the court.

The undertaking herein mentioned shall be understood to signify an agreement entered into by the complainant and the surety upon which a decree may be rendered in the same suit or proceeding against said complainant and surety, upon a hearing to assess damages of which hearing complainant and surety shall have reasonable notice, the said complainant and surety submitting themselves to the jurisdiction of the court for that purpose. But nothing herein contained shall deprive any party having a claim or cause of action under or upon such undertaking from electing to pursue his ordinary remedy by suit at law or in equity.

**Sec. 8. Noncompliance with obligations involved in labor disputes or failure to settle by negotiation or arbitration as preventing injunctive relief.**

No restraining order or injunctive relief shall be granted to any complainant who has failed to comply with any obligation imposed by law which is involved in the labor dispute in question, or who has failed to make every reasonable effort to settle such dispute either by negotiation or with the aid of any available governmental machinery of mediation or voluntary arbitration.

**Sec. 9. Granting of restraining order or injunction as dependent on previous findings of fact; limitation on prohibitions included in restraining orders and injunctions.**

No restraining order or temporary or permanent injunction shall be granted in a case involving or growing out of a labor dispute, except on the basis of findings of fact made and filed by the court in the record of the case prior to the issuance of such restraining order or injunction; and every restraining order or injunction granted in a case involving or growing out of a labor dispute shall include only a prohibition of such specific act or acts as may be expressly complained of in the bill of complaint or petition filed in such case and as shall be expressly included in said findings of fact made and filed by the court as provided herein.

**Sec. 10. Review by Court of Appeals of issuance or denial of temporary injunctions; record; precedence.**

Whenever any court of the United States shall issue or deny any temporary injunction in a case involving or growing out of a labor dispute, the court shall, upon the request of any party to the proceedings and on his filing the usual bond for costs, forthwith certify as in ordinary cases the record of the case to the court of appeals for its review. Upon the filing of such record in the court of appeals, the appeal shall be heard and the temporary injunctive order affirmed, modified, or set aside expeditiously.

**Sec. 11. Contempts; speedy and public trial; jury.**

In all cases arising under this Act in which a person shall be charged with contempt in a court of the United States (as herein defined), the accused shall enjoy the right to a speedy and public trial by an impartial jury of the State and district wherein the contempt shall have been committed: *Provided,* That this right shall not apply to contempts committed in the presence of the court or so near thereto as to interfere directly with the administration of justice or to apply to the misbehavior, misconduct, or disobedience of any officer of the court in respect to the writs, orders, or process of the court.*

**Sec. 12.* Contempts; demand for retirement of judge sitting in proceeding.**

The defendant in any proceeding for contempt of court may file with the court a demand for the retirement of the judge sitting in the

---

* Sections 11 and 12 were repealed by Act of June 25, 1948 (62 Stat. 862), a codification of the provisions of Title 18 of the United States Code. The substance of Section 11 was reenacted in the same Act (62 Stat. 844, 18 U.S.C. § 3692 (1970)); the substance of Section 12 is now found in Rules 42(a) and (b) of the Federal Rules of Criminal Procedure.

proceeding, if the contempt arises from an attack upon the character or conduct of such judge and if the attack occurred elsewhere than in the presence of the court or so near thereto as to interfere directly with the administration of justice. Upon the filing of any such demand the judge shall thereupon proceed no further, but another judge shall be designated in the same manner as is provided by law. The demand shall be filed prior to the hearing in the contempt proceeding.

### Sec. 13.   Definitions of terms and words used in chapter.

When used in this Act, and for the purposes of this Act—

(a)  A case shall be held to involve or to grow out of a labor dispute when the case involves persons who are engaged in the same industry, trade, craft, or occupation; or have direct or indirect interests therein; or who are employees of the same employer; or who are members of the same or an affiliated organization of employers or employees; whether such dispute is (1) between one or more employers or associations of employers and one or more employees or associations of employees; (2) between one or more employers or associations of employers and one or more employers or associations of employers; or (3) between one or more employees or associations of employees and one or more employees or associations of employees; or when the case involves any conflicting or competing interests in a "labor dispute" (as hereinafter defined) of "persons participating or interested" therein (as hereinafter defined).

(b)  A person or association shall be held to be a person participating or interested in a labor dispute if relief is sought against him or it, and if he or it is engaged in the same industry, trade, craft, or occupation in which such dispute occurs, or has a direct or indirect interest therein, or is a member, officer, or agent of any association composed in whole or in part of employers or employees engaged in such industry, trade, craft, or occupation.

(c)  The term "labor dispute" includes any controversy concerning terms or conditions of employment, or concerning the association or representation of persons in negotiating, fixing, maintaining, changing, or seeking to arrange terms or conditions of employment, regardless of whether or not the disputants stand in the proximate relation of employer and employee.

(d)  The term "court of the United States" means any court of the United States whose jurisdiction has been or may be conferred or defined or limited by Act of Congress, including the courts of the District of Columbia.

### Sec. 14. Separability of provisions.

If any provision of this Act or the application thereof to any person or circumstance is held unconstitutional or otherwise invalid, the remaining provisions of this Act and the application of such provisions to other persons or circumstances shall not be affected thereby.

### Sec. 15. Repeal of conflicting acts.

All acts and parts of acts in conflict with the provisions of this Act are repealed.

# RAILWAY LABOR ACT

44 Stat., Part II 577 (1926), as amended by 48 Stat. 1185 (1934), 49 Stat. 1189 (1936), 54 Stat. 785, 786 (1940), 64 Stat. 1238 (1951), 78 Stat. 748 (1964), 80 Stat. 208 (1966), and 84 Stat. 199 (1970);

45 U.S.C. §§ 151–88 (1982).

## TITLE I

### Sec. 1. Definitions.

When used in this Act and for the purposes of this Act—

First. The term "carrier" includes any express company, sleeping-car company, carrier by railroad, subject to the Interstate Commerce Act, and any company which is directly or indirectly owned or controlled by or under common control with any carrier by railroad and which operates any equipment or facilities or performs any service (other than trucking service) in connection with the transportation, receipt, delivery, elevation, transfer in transit, refrigeration or icing, storage, and handling of property transported by railroad, and any receiver, trustee, or other individual or body, judicial or otherwise, when in the possession of the business of any such "carrier": *Provided, however,* That the term "carrier" shall not include any street, interurban, or suburban electric railway, unless such railway is operating as a part of a general steam-railroad system of transportation, but shall not exclude any part of the general steam-railroad system of transportation now or hereafter operated by any other motive power. The Interstate Commerce Commission is authorized and directed upon request of the Mediation Board or upon complaint of any party interested to determine after hearing whether any line operated by electric power falls within the terms of this proviso. The term "carrier" shall not include any company by reason of its being engaged in the mining of coal, the supplying of coal to a carrier where delivery is not beyond the mine tipple, and the operation of equipment or facilities therefor, or in any of such activities.

Second. The term "Adjustment Board" means the National Railroad Adjustment Board created by this Act.

Third. The term "Mediation Board" means the National Mediation Board created by this Act.

Fourth. The term "commerce" means commerce among the several States or between any State, Territory, or the District of Columbia and any foreign nation, or between any Territory or the District of Columbia and any State, or between any Territory and any other Territory, or between any Territory and the District of Columbia, or within any Territory or the District of Columbia, or between points in the same State but through any other State or any Territory or the District of Columbia or any foreign nation.

Fifth. The term "employee" as used herein includes every person in the service of a carrier (subject to its continuing authority to supervise and direct the manner of rendition of his service) who performs any work defined as that of an employee or subordinate official in the orders of the Interstate Commerce Commission now in effect, and as the same may be amended or interpreted by orders hereafter entered by the Commission pursuant to the authority which is conferred upon it to enter orders amending or interpreting such existing orders: *Provided, however,* That no occupational classification made by order of the Interstate Commerce Commission shall be construed to define the crafts according to which railway employees may be organized by their voluntary action, nor shall the jurisdiction or powers of such employee organizations be regarded as in any way limited or defined by the provisions of this chapter or by the orders of the Commission.

The term "employee" shall not include any individual while such individual is engaged in the physical operations consisting of the mining of coal, the preparation of coal, the handling (other than movement by rail with standard railroad locomotives) of coal not beyond the mine tipple, or the loading of coal at the tipple.

Sixth. The term "representative" means any person or persons, labor union, organization, or corporation designated either by a carrier or group of carriers or by its or their employees, to act for it or them.

Seventh. The term "district court" includes the United States District Court for the District of Columbia; and the term "court of appeals" includes the United States Court of Appeals for the District of Columbia.

This Act may be cited as the "Railway Labor Act."

## Sec. 2. General purposes.

The purposes of the Act are: (1) To avoid any interruption to commerce or to the operation of any carrier engaged therein; (2) to forbid any limitation upon freedom of association among employees or any denial, as a condition of employment or otherwise, of the right of employees to join a labor organization; (3) to provide for the complete independence of carriers and of employees in the matter of self-organization to carry out the purposes of this chapter; (4) to provide for the prompt and orderly settlement of all disputes concerning rates of pay, rules, or working conditions; (5) to provide for the prompt and orderly settlement of all disputes growing out of grievances or out of the interpretation or application of agreements covering rates of pay, rules, or working conditions.

### General duties.

### First. Duty of carriers and employees to settle disputes.

It shall be the duty of all carriers, their officers, agents, and employees to exert every reasonable effort to make and maintain agreements concerning rates of pay, rules, and working conditions, and to settle all disputes, whether arising out of the application of such agreements or otherwise, in order to avoid any interruption to commerce or to the operation of any carrier growing out of any dispute between the carrier and the employees thereof.

### Second. Consideration of disputes by representatives.

All disputes between a carrier or carriers and its or their employees shall be considered, and, if possible, decided, with all expedition, in conference between representatives designated and authorized so to confer, respectively, by the carrier or carriers and by the employees thereof interested in the dispute.

### Third. Designation of representatives.

Representatives, for the purposes of this Act, shall be designated by the respective parties without interference, influence, or coercion by either party over the designation of representatives by the other; and neither party shall in any way interfere with, influence, or coerce the other in its choice of representatives. Representatives of employees for the purposes of this Act need not be persons in the employ of the carrier, and no carrier shall, by interference, influence, or coercion seek in any manner to prevent the designation by its employees as their representatives of those who or which are not employees of the carrier.

### Fourth. Organization and collective bargaining; freedom from interference by carrier; assistance in organizing or maintaining organization by carrier forbidden; deduction of dues from wages forbidden.

Employees shall have the right to organize and bargain collectively through representatives of their own choosing. The majority of any craft or class of employees shall have the right to determine who shall be the representative of the craft or class for the purposes of this Act. No carrier, its officers, or agents shall deny or in any way question the right of its employees to join, organize, or assist in organizing the labor organization of their choice, and it shall be unlawful for any carrier to interfere in any way with the organization of its employees, or to use the funds of the carrier in maintaining or assisting or contributing to any labor organization, labor representative, or other agency of collective bargaining, or in performing any work therefor, or to influence or coerce employees in an effort to induce them to join or remain or not to join or remain members of any labor organization, or to deduct from the wages of employees any dues, fees, assessments, or other contributions payable to labor organizations, or to collect or to assist in the collection of any such dues, fees, assessments, or other contributions: *Provided,* That nothing in this Act shall be construed to prohibit a carrier from permitting an employee, individually, or local representatives of employees from conferring with management during working hours without loss of time, or to prohibit a carrier from furnishing free transportation to its employees while engaged in the business of a labor organization.

### Fifth.   Agreements to join or not to join labor organizations forbidden.

No carrier, its officers, or agents shall require any person seeking employment to sign any contract or agreement promising to join or not to join a labor organization; and if any such contract has been enforced prior to the effective date of this Act, then such carrier shall notify the employees by an appropriate order that such contract has been discarded and is no longer binding on them in any way.

### Sixth.   Conference of representative;   time;   place;   private agreements.

In case of a dispute between a carrier or carriers and its or their employees, arising out of grievances or out of the interpretation or application of agreements concerning rates of pay, rules, or working conditions, it shall be the duty of the designated representative or representatives of such carrier or carriers and of such employees, within ten days after the receipt of notice of a desire on the part of either party to confer in respect to such dispute, to specify a time and place at which such conference shall be held: *Provided,* (1) That the place so specified shall be situated upon the line of the carrier involved or as otherwise mutually agreed upon; and (2) that the time so specified shall allow the designated conferees reasonable opportunity to reach such place of conference, but shall not exceed twenty days from the receipt of such notice: *And provided further,* That nothing in this Act shall be construed to supersede the provisions of any agreement (as to conferences) then in effect between the parties.

### Seventh.   Change in pay, rules, or working conditions contrary to agreement or to section 6 forbidden.

No carrier, its officers, or agents shall change the rates of pay, rules, or working conditions of its employees, as a class, as embodied in agreements except in the manner prescribed in such agreements or in section 6 of this Act.

### Eighth.   Notices of manner of settlement of disputes; posting.

Every carrier shall notify its employees by printed notices in such form and posted at such times and places as shall be specified by the Mediation Board that all disputes between the carrier and its employees will be handled in accordance with the requirements of this Act, and in such notices there shall be printed verbatim, in large type, the third, fourth, and fifth paragraphs of this section. The provisions of said paragraphs are made a part of the contract of employment between the carrier and each employee, and shall be held binding upon the parties, regardless of any other express or implied agreements between them.

### Ninth.  Disputes as to identity of representatives; designation by Mediation Board; secret elections.

If any dispute shall arise among a carrier's employees as to who are the representatives of such employees designated and authorized in accordance with the requirements of this Act, it shall be the duty of the Mediation Board, upon request of either party to the dispute, to investigate such dispute and to certify to both parties, in writing, within thirty days after the receipt of the invocation of its services, the name or names of the individuals or organizations that have been designated and authorized to represent the employees involved in the dispute, and certify the same to the carrier. Upon receipt of such certification the carrier shall treat with the representative so certified as the representative of the craft or class for the purposes of this Act. In such an investigation, the Mediation Board shall be authorized to take a secret ballot of the employees involved, or to utilize any other appropriate method of ascertaining the names of their duly designated and authorized representatives in such manner as shall insure the choice of representatives by the employees without interference, influence, or coercion exercised by the carrier. In the conduct of any election for the purposes herein indicated the Board shall designate who may participate in the election and establish the rules to govern the election, or may appoint a committee of three neutral persons who after hearing shall within ten days designate the employees who may participate in the election. The Board shall have access to and have power to make copies of the books and records of the carriers to obtain and utilize such information as may be deemed necessary by it to carry out the purposes and provisions of this paragraph.

### Tenth.  Violations; prosecution and penalties.

The willful failure or refusal of any carrier, its officers or agents, to comply with the terms of the third, fourth, fifth, seventh, or eighth paragraph of this section shall be a misdemeanor, and upon conviction thereof the carrier, officer, or agent offending shall be subject to a fine of not less than $1,000, nor more than $20,000, or imprisonment for not more than six months, or both fine and imprisonment, for each offense, and each day during which such carrier, officer, or agent shall willfully fail or refuse to comply with the terms of the said paragraphs of this section shall constitute a separate offense. It shall be the duty of any United States attorney to whom any duly designated representative of a carrier's employees may apply to institute in the proper court and to prosecute under the direction of the Attorney, General of the United States, all necessary proceedings for the enforcement of the provisions of this section, and for the punishment of all violations thereof and the costs and expenses of such prosecution shall be paid out of the appropriation for the expenses of the courts of the United States: *Provided,* That nothing in this Act shall be construed to require an individual employee to render labor or service without his consent, nor shall anything in this Act be construed to make the quitting of his labor by an individual employee an illegal act; nor shall any court issue any process to compel the performance by an individual employee of such labor or service, without his consent.

**Eleventh.  Union security agreements; check-off.**

Notwithstanding any other provisions of this Act, or of any other statute or law of the United States, or Territory thereof, or of any State, any carrier or carriers as defined in this Act and a labor organization or labor organizations duly designated and authorized to represent employees in accordance with the requirements of this Act shall be permitted—

(a)  to make agreements, requiring, as a condition of continued employment, that within sixty days following the beginning of such employment, or the effective date of such agreements, whichever is the later, all employees shall become members of the labor organization representing their craft or class: *Provided,* That no such agreement shall require such condition of employment with respect to employees to whom membership is not available upon the same terms and conditions as are generally applicable to any other member or with respect to employees to whom membership was denied or terminated for any reason other than the failure of the employee to tender the periodic dues, initiation fees, and assessments (not including fines and penalties) uniformly required as a condition of acquiring or retaining membership.

(b)  to make agreements providing for the deduction by such carrier or carriers from the wages of its or their employees in a craft or class and payment to the labor organization representing the craft or class of such employees, of any periodic dues, initiation fees, and assessments (not including fines and penalties) uniformly required as a condition of acquiring or retaining membership: *Provided,* That no such agreement shall be effective with respect to any individual employee until he shall have furnished the employer with a written assignment to the labor organization of such membership dues, initiation fees, and assessments, which shall be revocable in writing after the expiration of one year or upon the termination date of the applicable collective agreement, whichever occurs sooner.

(c) The requirement of membership in a labor organization in an agreement made pursuant to subparagraph (a) of this paragraph shall be satisfied, as to both a present or future employee in engine, train, yard, or hostling service, that is, an employee engaged in any of the services or capacities covered in the First division of paragraph (h) of section 3 of this Act defining the jurisdictional scope of the First Division of the National Railroad Adjustment Board, if said employee shall hold or acquire membership in any one of the labor organizations, national in scope, organized in accordance with this Act and admitting to membership employees of a craft or class in any of said services; and no agreement made pursuant to subparagraph (b) of this paragraph shall provide for deductions from his wages for periodic dues, initiation fees, or assessments payable to any labor organization other than that in which he holds membership: *Provided, however,* That as to an employee in any of said services on a particular carrier at the effective date of any such agreement on a carrier, who is not a member of any one of the labor organizations, national in scope, organized in accordance with this Act and admitting to membership employees of a craft or class in any of said services, such employee, as a condition of continuing his employment, may be required to become a member of the organization representing the craft in which he is employed on the effective date of the first agreement applicable to him: *Provided, further,* That nothing herein or in any such agreement or agreements shall prevent an employee from changing membership from one organization to another organization admitting to membership employees of a craft or class in any of said services.

(d) Any provisions in paragraphs Fourth and Fifth of this section in conflict herewith are to the extent of such conflict amended.

### Sec. 3. National Railroad Adjustment Board.

**First. Establishment; composition; powers and duties; divisions; hearings and awards; judicial review.**

There is established a Board, to be known as the "National Railroad Adjustment Board", the members of which shall be selected within thirty days after June 21, 1934, and it is provided—

(a) That the said Adjustment Board shall consist of thirty-four members, seventeen of whom shall be selected by the carriers and seventeen by such labor organizations of the employees, national in scope, as have been or may be organized in accordance with the provisions of section 2 of this Act.

(b) The carriers, acting each through its board of directors or its receiver or receivers, trustee or trustees, or through an officer or officers designated for that purpose by such board, trustee or trustees, or receiver or receivers, shall prescribe the rules under which its representatives shall be selected and shall select the representatives of the carriers on the Adjustment Board and designate the division on which each such representatives shall serve, but no carrier or system of carriers shall have more than one voting representative on any division of the Board.

(c) Except as provided in the second paragraph of subsection (h) of this section, the national labor organizations, as defined in paragraph (a) of this section, acting each through the chief executive or other medium designated by the organization or association thereof, shall prescribe the rules under which the labor members of the Adjustment Board shall be selected and shall select such members and designate the division on which each member shall serve; but no labor organization shall have more than one voting representative on any division of the Board.

(d) In case of a permanent or temporary vacancy on the Adjustment Board, the vacancy shall be filled by selection in the same manner as in the original selection.

(e) If either the carriers or the labor organizations of the employees fail to select and designate representatives to the Adjustment Board, as provided in paragraphs (b) and (c) of this section, respectively, within sixty days after June 21, 1934, in case of any original appointment to office of a member of the Adjustment Board, or in case of a vacancy in any such office within thirty days after such vacancy occurs, the Mediation Board shall thereupon directly make the appointment and shall select an individual associated in interest with the carriers or the group of labor organizations of employees, whichever he is to represent.

(f) In the event a dispute arises as to the right of any national labor organization to participate as per paragraph (c) of this section in the selection and designation of the labor members of the Adjustment Board, the Secretary of Labor shall investigate the claim of such labor organization to participate, and if such claim in the judgment of the Secretary of Labor has merit, the Secretary shall notify the Mediation Board accordingly, and within ten days after receipt of such advice the Mediation Board shall request those national labor organizations duly qualified as per paragraph (c) of this section to participate in the selection and designation of the labor members of the Adjustment Board to select a representative. Such representative, together with a representative likewise designated by the claimant, and a third or neutral party designated by the Mediation Board, constituting a board of three, shall within thirty days after the appointment of the neutral member, investigate the claims of the labor organization desiring participation and decide whether or not it was organized in accordance with section 2 hereof and is otherwise properly qualified to participate in the selection of the labor members of the Adjustment Board, and the findings of such boards of three shall be final and binding.

(g) Each member of the Adjustment Board shall be compensated by the party or parties he is to represent. Each third or neutral party selected under the provisions of paragraph (f) of this section shall receive from the Mediation Board such compensation as the Mediation Board may fix, together with his necessary traveling expenses and expenses actually incurred for subsistence, or per diem allowance in lieu thereof, subject to the provisions of law applicable thereto, while serving as such third or neutral party.

(h) The said Adjustment Board shall be composed of four divisions, whose proceedings shall be independent of one another, and the said divisions as well as the number of their members shall be as follows:

First division: To have jurisdiction over disputes involving train- and yard-service employees of carriers; that is, engineers, firemen, hostlers, and outside hostler helpers, conductors, trainmen, and yard-service employees. This division shall consist of eight members, four of whom shall be selected and designated by the carriers and four of whom shall be selected and designated by the national labor organizations, national in scope and organized in accordance with section 2 hereof and which represent employees in engine, train, yard, or hostling service: *Provided, however,* That each labor organization shall select and designate two members on the First Division and that no labor organization shall have more than one vote in any proceedings of the First Division or in the adoption of any award with respect to any dispute submitted to the First Division: *Provided further, however,* That the carrier members of the First Division shall cast no more than two votes in any proceeding of the division or in the adoption of any award with respect to any dispute submitted to the First Division.

Second division: To have jurisdiction over disputes involving machinists, boilermakers, blacksmiths, sheet-metal workers, electrical workers, carmen, the helpers and apprentices of all the foregoing, coach cleaners, power-house employees, and railroad-shop laborers. This division shall consist of ten members, five of whom shall be selected by the carriers and five by the national labor organizations of the employees.

Third division: To have jurisdiction over disputes involving station, tower, and telegraph employees, train dispatchers, maintenance-of-way men, clerical employees, freight handlers, express, station, and store employees, signal men, sleeping-car conductors, sleeping-car porters, and maids and dining-car employees. This division shall consist of ten members, five of whom shall be selected by the carriers and five by the national labor organizations of employees.

Fourth division: To have jurisdiction over disputes involving employees of carriers directly or indirectly engaged in transportation of passengers or property by water, and all other employees of carriers over which jurisdiction is not given to the first, second, and third divisions. This division shall consist of six members, three of whom shall be selected by the carriers and three by the national labor organizations of the employees.

(i) The disputes between an employee or group of employees and a carrier or carriers growing out of grievances or out of the interpretation or application of agreements concerning rates of pay, rules, or working conditions, including cases pending and unadjusted on June 21, 1934, shall be handled in the usual manner up to and including the chief operating officer of the carrier designated to handle such disputes; but, failing to reach an adjustment in this manner, the disputes may be referred by petition of the parties or by either party to the appropriate division of the Adjustment Board with a full statement of the facts and all supporting data bearing upon the disputes.

(j) Parties may be heard either in person, by counsel, or by other representatives, as they may respectively elect, and the several divisions of the Adjustment Board shall give due notice of all hearings to the employee or employees and the carrier or carriers involved in any disputes submitted to them.

(k) Any division of the Adjustment Board shall have authority to empower two or more of its members to conduct hearings and make findings upon disputes, when properly submitted, at any place designated by the division: *Provided, however,* That except as provided in paragraph (h) of this section, final awards as to any such dispute must be made by the entire division as hereinafter provided.

(*l*) Upon failure of any division to agree upon an award because of a deadlock or inability to secure a majority vote of the division members, as provided in paragraph (n) of this section, then such division shall forthwith agree upon and select a neutral person, to be known as "referee", to sit with the division as a member thereof, and make an award. Should the division fail to agree upon and select a referee within ten days of the date of the deadlock or inability to secure a majority vote, then the division, or any member thereof, or the parties or either party to the dispute may certify that fact to the Mediation Board, which

Board shall, within ten days from the date of receiving such certificate, select and name the referee to sit with the division as a member thereof and make an award. The Mediation Board shall be bound by the same provisions in the appointment of these neutral referees as are provided elsewhere in this Act for the appointment of arbitrators and shall fix and pay the compensation of such referees.

(m) The awards of the several divisions of the Adjustment Board shall be stated in writing. A copy of the awards shall be furnished to the respective parties to the controversy, and the awards shall be final and binding upon both parties to the dispute. In case a dispute arises involving an interpretation of the award, the division of the Board upon request of either party shall interpret the award in the light of the dispute.

(n) A majority vote of all members of the division of the Adjustment Board eligible to vote shall be competent to make an award with respect to any dispute submitted to it.

(o) In case of an award by any division of the Adjustment Board in favor of petitioner, the division of the Board shall make an order, directed to the carrier, to make the award effective and, if the award includes a requirement for the payment of money, to pay to the employee the sum to which he is entitled under the award on or before a day named. In the event any division determines that an award favorable to the petitioner should not be made in any dispute referred to it, the division shall make an order to the petitioner stating such determination.

(p) If a carrier does not comply with an order of a division of the Adjustment Board within the time limit in such order, the petitioner, or any person for whose benefit such order was made, may file in the District Court of the United States for the district in which he resides or in which is located the principal operating office of the carrier, or through which the carrier operates, a petition setting forth briefly the causes for which he claims relief, and the order of the division of the Adjustment Board in the premises. Such suit in the District Court of the United States shall proceed in all respects as other civil suits, except that on the trial of such suit the findings and order of the division of the Adjustment Board shall be conclusive on the parties, and except that the petitioner shall not be liable for costs in the district court nor for costs at any subsequent stage of the proceedings, unless they accrue upon his appeal, and such costs shall be paid out of the appropriation for the expenses of the courts of the United States. If the petitioner shall finally prevail he shall be allowed a reasonable attorney's fee, to be taxed and collected as a part of the costs of the suit. The district courts are empowered, under the rules of the court governing actions at law, to make such order and enter such judgment, by writ of mandamus or otherwise, as may be appropriate to enforce or set aside the order of the division of the Adjustment Board: *Provided, however,* That such order may not be set aside except for failure of the division to comply with the requirements of this Act, for failure of the order to conform, or confine itself, to matters within the scope of the division's jurisdiction, or for fraud or corruption by a member of the division making the order.

(q) If any employee or group of employees, or any carrier, is aggrieved by the failure of any division of the Adjustment Board to make an award in a dispute referred to it, or is aggrieved by any of the terms of an award or by the failure of the division to include certain terms in such award, then such employee or group of employees or carrier may file in any United States district court in which a petition under paragraph (p) could be filed, a petition for review of the division's order. A copy of the petition shall be forthwith transmitted by the clerk of the court to the Adjustment Board. The Adjustment Board shall file in the court the record of the proceedings on which it based its action. The court shall have jurisdiction to affirm the order of the division, or to set it aside, in whole or in part, or it may remand the proceeding to the division for such further action as it may direct. On such review, the findings and order of the division shall be conclusive on the parties, except that the order of the division may be set aside, in whole or in part, or remanded to the division, for failure of the division to comply with the requirements of this Act, for failure of the order to conform, or confine itself, to matters within the scope of the division's jurisdiction, or for fraud or corruption by a member of the division making the order. The judgment of the court shall be subject to review as provided in sections 1291 and 1254 of title 28, United States Code.

(r) All actions at law based upon the provisions of this section shall be begun within two years from the time the cause of action accrues under the award of the division of the Adjustment Board, and not after.

(s) The several divisions of the Adjustment Board shall maintain headquarters in Chicago, Illinois, meet regularly, and continue in session so long as there is pending before the division any matter within its jurisdiction which has been submitted for its consideration and which has not been disposed of.

(t) Whenever practicable, the several divisions or subdivisions of the Adjustment Board shall be supplied with suitable quarters in any Federal building located at its place of meeting.

(u) The Adjustment Board may, subject to the approval of the Mediation Board, employ and fix the compensations of such assistants as it deems necessary in carrying on its proceedings.

The compensation of such employees shall be paid by the Mediation Board.

(v) The Adjustment Board shall meet within forty days after June 21, 1934, and adopt such rules as it deems necessary to control proceedings before the respective divisions and not in conflict with the provisions of this section. Immediately following the meeting of the entire Board and the adoption of such rules, the respective divisions shall meet and organize by the selection of a chairman, a vice chairman, and a secretary. Thereafter each division shall annually designate one of its members to act as chairman and one of its members to act as vice chairman: *Provided, however,* That the chairmanship and vice-chairmanship of any division shall alternate as between the groups, so that both the chairmanship and vice-chairmanship shall be held alternately by a representative of the carriers and a representative of the employees. In case of a vacancy, such vacancy shall be filled for the unexpired term by the selection of a successor from the same group.

(w) Each division of the Adjustment Board shall annually prepare and submit a report of its activities to the Mediation Board, and the substance of such report shall be included in the annual report of the Mediation Board to the Congress of the United States. The reports of each division of the Adjustment Board and the annual report of the Mediation Board shall state in detail all cases heard, all actions taken, the names, salaries, and duties of all agencies, employees, and officers receiving compensation from the United States under the authority of this chapter, and an account of all moneys appropriated by Congress pursuant to the authority conferred by this Act and disbursed by such agencies, employees, and officers.

(x) Any division of the Adjustment Board shall have authority, in its discretion, to establish regional adjustment boards to act in its place and stead for each limited period as such division may determine to be necessary. Carrier members of such regional boards shall be designated in keeping with rules devised for this purpose by the carrier members of the Adjustment Board and the labor members shall be designated in keeping with rules devised for this purpose by the labor members of the Adjustment Board. Any such regional board shall, during the time for which it is appointed, have the same authority to conduct hearings, make findings upon disputes and adopt the same procedure as the division of the Adjustment Board appointing it, and its decisions shall be enforceable to the same extent and under the same processes. A neutral person, as referee, shall be appointed for service in connection with any such regional adjustment board in the same circumstances and manner as provided in paragraph (*l*) of this section, with respect to a division of the Adjustment Board.

**Second.** **System, group, or regional boards: establishment by voluntary agreement; special adjustment boards: establishment, composition, designation of representatives by Mediation Board, neutral member, compensation, quorum, finality and enforcement of awards.**

Nothing in this section shall be construed to prevent any individual carrier, system, or group of carriers and any class or classes of its or their employees, all acting through their representatives, selected in accordance with the provisions of this Act, from mutually agreeing to the establishment of a system, group, or regional boards of adjustment for the purpose of adjusting and deciding disputes of the character specified in this section. In the event that either party to such a system, group, or regional board of adjustment is dissatisfied with such arrangement, it may upon ninety days' notice to the other party elect to come under the jurisdiction of the Adjustment Board.

If written request is made upon any individual carrier by the representative of any craft or class of employees of such carrier for the establishment of a special board of adjustment to resolve disputes otherwise referable to the Adjustment Board, or any dispute which has been pending before the Adjustment Board for twelve months from the date the dispute (claim) is received by the Board, or if any carrier makes such a request upon any such representative, the carrier or the representative upon whom such request is made shall join in an agreement establishing such a board within thirty days from the date such request is made. The cases which may be considered by such board shall be defined in the agreement establishing it. Such board shall consist of one person designated by the carrier and one person designated by the representative of the employees. If such carrier or such representative fails to agree upon the establishment of such a board as provided herein, or to exercise its rights to designate a member of the board, the carrier or representative making the request for the establishment of the special board may request the Mediation Board to designate a member of the special board on behalf of the carrier or representative upon whom such request was made. Upon receipt of a request for such designation the Mediation Board shall promptly make such designation and shall select an individual associated in interest with the carrier or representative he is to represent, who, with the member appointed by the carrier or representative requesting the establishment of the special board, shall constitute the board. Each member of the board shall be compensated by the party he is to represent. The members of the board so designated shall determine all matters not previously agreed upon by the carrier and the representative of the employees with respect to the establishment and jurisdiction of the board. If they are unable to agree such matters shall be determined by a neutral member of the board selected or appointed and compensated in the same manner as is hereinafter provided with respect to situations where the members of the board are unable to agree upon an award. Such neutral member shall cease to be a member of the board when he has determined such matters. If with respect to any dispute or group of disputes the members of the board designated by the carrier and the representative are unable to agree upon an award disposing of the dispute or group of disputes they shall by mutual agreement select a neutral person to be a member of the board for the consideration and disposition of such dispute or group of disputes. In the event the members of the board designated by the parties are unable, within ten days after their failure to agree upon an award, to agree upon the selection of such neutral person, either member of the board may request the Mediation Board to appoint such neutral person and upon receipt of such request the Mediation Board shall promptly make such appointment. The neutral person so selected or appointed shall be compensated and reimbursed for expenses by the Mediation Board. Any two members of the board shall be competent to render an award. Such awards shall be final and binding upon both parties to the dispute and if in favor of the petitioner, shall direct the other party to comply therewith on or before the day named. Compliance with such awards shall be enforcible by proceedings in the United States district courts in the same manner and subject to the same provisions that apply to proceedings for enforcement of compliance with awards of the Adjustment Board.

### Sec. 4. National Mediation Board.

**First. Board of Mediation abolished; National Mediation Board established; composition; term of office; qualifications; salaries; removal.**

The Board of Mediation is abolished, effective thirty days from June 21, 1934, and the members, secretary, officers, assistants, employees, and agents thereof, in office upon June 21, 1934, shall continue to function and receive their salaries for a period of thirty days from such date in the same manner as though this Act had not been passed. There is established, as an independent agency in the executive branch of the Government, a board to be known as the "National Mediation Board", to be composed of three members appointed by the President, by and with the advice and consent of the Senate, not more than two of whom shall be of the same political party. Each member of the Mediation Board in office on January 1, 1965, shall be deemed to have been appointed for a term of office which shall expire on July 1 of the year his term would have otherwise expired. The terms of office of all successors shall expire three years after the expiration of the terms for which their predecessors were appointed; but any member appointed to fill a vacancy occurring prior to the expiration of the term for which his predecessor was appointed shall be appointed only for the unexpired term of his predecessor. Vacancies in the Board shall not impair the powers nor affect the duties of the Board nor of the remaining members of the Board. Two of the members in office shall constitute a quorum for the transaction of the business of the Board. Each member of the Board shall receive necessary traveling and subsistence expenses, or per diem allowance in lieu thereof, subject to the provisions of law applicable thereto, while away from the principal office of the Board on business required by this Act.* No person in the employment of or who is pecuniarily or otherwise interested in any organization of employees or any carrier shall enter upon the duties of or continue to be a member of the Board. Upon the expiration of his term of office a member shall continue to serve until his successor is appointed and shall have qualified.

All cases referred to the Board of Mediation and unsettled on June 21, 1934, shall be handled to conclusion by the Mediation Board.

A member of the Board may be removed by the President for inefficiency, neglect of duty, malfeasance in office, or ineligibility, but for no other cause.

**Second. Chairman; principal office; delegation of powers; oaths; seal; report.**

The Mediation Board shall annually designate a member to act as chairman. The Board shall maintain its principal office in the District of Columbia, but it may meet at any other place whenever it deems it necessary so to do. The Board may designate one or more of its members to exercise the functions of the Board in mediation proceedings. Each member of the Board shall have power to administer oaths and affirmations. The Board shall have a seal which shall be judicially noticed. The Board shall make an annual report to Congress.

**Third. Appointment of experts and other employees; salaries of employees; expenditures.**

The Mediation Board may (1) subject to the civil service laws, appoint such experts and assistants to act in a confidential capacity and such other officers and employees as are essential to the effective transaction of the work of the Board; (2) in accordance with the Classification Act of 1949, fix the salaries of such experts, assistants, officers, and employees; and (3) make such expenditures (including expenditures for rent and personal services at the seat of government and elsewhere, for law books, periodicals, and books of reference, and for printing and binding, and including expenditures for salaries and compensation, necessary traveling expenses and expenses actually incured for subsistence, and other necessary expenses of the Mediation Board, Adjustment Board, Regional Adjustment Boards established under paragraph [x] of section 3 of this Act, and boards of arbitration, in accordance with the provisions of this section and sections 3

---

* Each Board member also receives a salary, currently (as of January 1, 1984) in the amount of $69,600 per year; the salary of the Board Chairman is $70,800 per year. See 5 U.S.C.A. §§ 5314, 5315 (and note following) (West Supp. 1985).

and 7 of this Act, respectively), as may be necessary for the execution of the functions vested in the Board, in the Adjustment Board and in the boards of arbitration, and as may be provided for by the Congress from time to time. All expenditures of the Board shall be allowed and paid on the presentation of itemized vouchers therefor approved by the chairman.

**Fourth.   Delegation of powers and duties.**

The Mediation Board is authorized by its order to assign, or refer, any portion of its work, business, or functions arising under this or any other Act of Congress, or referred to it by Congress or either branch thereof, to an individual member of the Board or to an employee or employees of the Board to be designated by such order for action thereon, and by its order at any time to amend, modify, supplement, or rescind any such assignment or reference. All such orders shall take effect forthwith and remain in effect until otherwise ordered by the Board. In conformity with and subject to the order or orders of the Mediation Board in the premises, [any] such individual member of the Board or employee designated shall have power and authority to act as to any of said work, business, or functions so assigned or referred to him for action by the Board.

**Fifth.   Transfer of officers and employees of Board of Mediation; transfer of appropriation.**

All officers and employees of the Board of Mediation (except the members thereof, whose offices are abolished) whose services in the judgment of the Mediation Board are necessary to the efficient operation of the Board are transferred to the Board, without change in classification or compensation; except that the Board may provide for the adjustment of such classification or compensation to conform to the duties to which such officers and employees may be assigned.

All unexpended appropriations for the operation of the Board of Mediation that are available at the time of the abolition of the Board of Mediation shall be transferred to the Mediation Board and shall be available for its use for salaries and other authorized expenditures.

### Sec. 5.   Functions of Mediation Board.

**First.   Disputes within jurisdiction of Mediation Board.**

The parties, or either party, to a dispute between an employee or group of employees and a carrier may invoke the services of the Mediation Board in any of the following cases:

(a) A dispute concerning changes in rates of pay, rules, or working conditions not adjusted by the parties in conference.

(b) Any other dispute not referable to the National Railroad Adjustment Board and not adjusted in conference between the parties or where conferences are refused.

The Mediation Board may proffer its services in case any labor emergency is found by it to exist at any time.

In either event the said Board shall promptly put itself in communication with the parties to such controversy, and shall use its best efforts, by mediation, to bring them to agreement. If such efforts to bring about an amicable settlement through mediation shall be unsuccessful, the said Board shall at once endeavor as its final required action (except as provided in paragraph third of this section and in section 10 of this Act) to induce the parties to submit their controversy to arbitration, in accordance with the provisions of this Act.

If arbitration at the request of the Board shall be refused by one or both parties, the Board shall at once notify both parties in writing that its mediatory efforts have failed and for thirty days thereafter, unless in the intervening period the parties agree to arbitration, or an emergency board shall be created under section 10 of this Act, no change shall be made in the rates of pay, rules, or working conditions or established practices in effect prior to the time the dispute arose.

**Second. Interpretation of agreement.**

In any case in which a controversy arises over the meaning or the application of any agreement reached through mediation under the provisions of this Act, either party to the said agreement, or both, may apply to the Mediation Board for an interpretation of the meaning or application of such agreement. The said Board shall upon receipt of such request notify the parties to the controversy, and after a hearing of both sides give its interpretation within thirty days.

**Third. Duties of Board with respect to arbitration of disputes; arbitrators; acknowledgment of agreement; notice to arbitrators; reconvening of arbitrators; filing contracts with Board; custody of records and documents.**

The Mediation Board shall have the following duties with respect to the arbitration of disputes under section 7 of this Act:

(a) On failure of the arbitrators named by the parties to agree on the remaining arbitrator or arbitrators within the time set by section 7 of this Act, it shall be the duty of the Mediation Board to name such remaining arbitrator or arbitrators. It shall be the duty of the Board in naming such arbitrator or arbitrators to appoint only those whom the Board shall deem wholly disinterested in the controversy to be arbitrated and impartial and without bias as between the parties to such arbitration. Should, however, the Board name an arbitrator or arbitrators not so disinterested and impartial then, upon proper investigation and presentation of the facts, the Board shall promptly remove such arbitrator.

If an arbitrator named by the Mediation Board, in accordance with the provisions of this Act, shall be removed by such Board as provided by this Act, or if such an arbitrator refuses or is unable to serve, it shall be the duty of the Mediation Board, promptly, to select another arbitrator, in the same manner as provided in this Act for an original appointment by the Mediation Board.

(b) Any member of the Mediation Board is authorized to take the acknowledgment of an agreement to arbitrate under this Act. When so acknowledged, or when acknowledged by the parties before a notary public or the clerk of a district court or a court of appeals of the United States, such agreement to arbitrate shall be delivered to a member of said Board or transmitted to said Board, to be filed in its office.

(c) When an agreement to arbitrate has been filed with the Mediation Board, or with one of its members, as provided by this section, and when the said Board has been furnished the names of the arbitrators chosen by the parties to the controversy it shall be the duty of the Board to cause a notice in writing to be served upon said arbitrators, notifying them of their appointment, requesting them to meet promptly to name the remaining arbitrator or arbitrators necessary to complete the Board of Arbitration, and advising them of the period within which, as provided by the agreement to arbitrate, they are empowered to name such arbitrator or arbitrators.

(d) Either party to an arbitration desiring the reconvening of a board of arbitration to pass upon any controversy arising over the meaning or application of an award may so notify the Mediation Board in writing, stating in such notice the question or questions to be submitted to such reconvened Board. The Mediation Board shall thereupon promptly communicate with the members of the Board of Arbitration, or a subcommittee of such Board appointed for such purpose pursuant to a provision in the agreement to arbitrate, and arrange for the reconvening of said Board of Arbitration or subcommittee, and shall notify the respective parties to the controversy of the time and place at which the Board, or the subcommittee, will meet for hearings upon the matters in controversy to be submitted to it. No evidence other than that contained in the record filed with the original award shall be received or considered by such reconvened Board or subcommittee, except such evidence as may be necessary to illustrate the interpretations suggested by the parties. If any member of the original Board is unable or unwilling to serve on such reconvened Board or subcommittee thereof, another arbitrator shall be named in the same manner and with the same powers and duties as such original arbitrator.

(e) Within sixty days after June 21, 1934, every carrier shall file with the Mediation Board a copy of each contract with its employees in effect on the 1st day of April 1934, covering rates of pay, rules, and working conditions. If no contract with any craft or class of its employees has been entered into, the carrier shall file with the

Mediation Board a statement of that fact, including also a statement of the rates of pay, rules, and working conditions applicable in dealing with such craft or class. When any new contract is executed or change is made in an existing contract with any class or craft of its employees covering rates of pay, rules, or working conditions, or in those rates of pay, rules, and working conditions of employees not covered by contract, the carrier shall file the same with the Mediation Board within thirty days after such new contract or change in existing contract has been executed or rates of pay, rules, and working conditions have been made effective.

(f) The Mediation Board shall be the custodian of all papers and documents heretofore filed with or transferred to the Board of Mediation bearing upon the settlement, adjustment, or determination of disputes between carriers and their employees or upon mediation or arbitration proceedings held under or pursuant to the provisions of any Act of Congress in respect thereto; and the President is authorized to designate a custodian of the records and property of the Board of Mediation until the transfer and delivery of such records to the Mediation Board and to require the transfer and delivery to the Mediation Board of any and all such papers and documents filed with it or in its possession.

### Sec. 6. Procedure in changing rates of pay, rules, and working conditions.

Carriers and representatives of the employees shall give at least thirty days' written notice of an intended change in agreements affecting rates of pay, rules, or working conditions, and the time and place for the beginning of conference between the representatives of the parties interested in such intended changes shall be agreed upon within ten days after the receipt of said notice, and said time shall be within the thirty days provided in the notice. In every case where such notice of intended change has been given, or conferences are being held with reference thereto, or the services of the Mediation Board have been requested by either party, or said Board has proffered its services, rates of pay, rules, or working conditions shall not be altered by the carrier until the controversy has been finally acted upon, as required by section 5 of this Act, by the Mediation Board, unless a period of ten days has elapsed after termination of conferences without request for or proffer of the services of the Mediation Board.

### Sec. 7. Arbitration.

#### First. Submission of controversy to arbitration.

Whenever a controversy shall arise between a carrier or carriers and its or their employees which is not settled either in conference between representatives of the parties or by the appropriate adjustment board or through mediation, in the manner provided in sections

1–6 of this Act such controversy may, by agreement of the parties to such controversy, be submitted to the arbitration of a board of three (or, if the parties to the controversy so stipulate, of six) persons: *Provided, however,* That the failure or refusal of either party to submit a controversy to arbitration shall not be construed as a violation of any legal obligation imposed upon such party by the terms of this Act or otherwise.

**Second.    Manner of selecting board of arbitration.**

Such board of arbitration shall be chosen in the following manner:

(a)  In the case of a board of three the carrier or carriers and the representatives of the employees, parties respectively to the agreement to arbitrate, shall each name one arbitrator; the two arbitrators thus chosen shall select a third arbitrator.  If the arbitrators chosen by the parties shall fail to name the third arbitrator within five days after their first meeting, such third arbitrator shall be named by the Mediation Board.

(b)  In the case of a board of six the carrier or carriers and the representatives of the employees, parties respectively to the agreement to arbitrate, shall each name two arbitrators; the four arbitrators thus chosen shall, by a majority vote, select the remaining two arbitrators.  If the arbitrators chosen by the parties shall fail to name the two arbitrators within fifteen days after their first meeting, the said two arbitrators, or as many of them as have not been named, shall be named by the Mediation Board.

**Third.    Board of arbitration; organization; compensation; procedure.**

**(a)  Notice of selection or failure to select arbitrators.**

When the arbitrators selected by the respective parties have agreed upon the remaining arbitrator or arbitrators, they shall notify the Mediation Board; and, in the event of their failure to agree upon any or upon all of the necessary arbitrators within the period fixed by this Act, they shall, at the expiration of such period, notify the Mediation Board of the arbitrators selected, if any, or of their failure to make or to complete such selection.

**(b)  Organization of board; procedure.**

The board of arbitration shall organize and select its own chairman and make all necessary rules for conducting its hearings: *Provided, however,* That the board of arbitration shall be bound to give the parties to the controversy a full and fair hearing, which shall include an opportunity to present evidence in support of their claims, and an opportunity to present their case in person, by counsel, or by other representative as they may respectively elect.

### (c) Duty to reconvene; questions considered.

Upon notice from the Mediation Board that the parties, or either party, to an arbitration desire the reconvening of the board of arbitration (or a subcommittee of such board of arbitration appointed for such purpose pursuant to the agreement to arbitrate) to pass upon any controversy over the meaning or application of their award, the board, or its subcommittee, shall at once reconvene. No question other than, or in addition to, the questions relating to the meaning or application of the award, submitted by the party or parties in writing, shall be considered by the reconvened board of arbitration or its subcommittee.

Such rulings shall be acknowledged by such board or subcommittee thereof in the same manner, and filed in the same district court clerk's office, as the original award and become a part thereof.

### (d) Competency of arbitrators.

No arbitrator, except those chosen by the Mediation Board, shall be incompetent to act as an arbitrator because of his interest in the controversy to be arbitrated, or because of his connection with or partiality to either of the parties to the arbitration.

### (e) Compensation and expenses.

Each member of any board of arbitration created under the provisions of this Act named by either party to the arbitration shall be compensated by the party naming him. Each arbitrator selected by the arbitrators or named by the Mediation Board shall receive from the Mediation Board such compensation as the Mediation Board may fix, together with his necessary traveling expenses and expenses actually incurred for subsistence, while serving as an arbitrator.

### (f) Award; disposition of original and copies.

The board of arbitration shall furnish a certified copy of its award to the respective parties to the controversy, and shall transmit the original, together with the papers and proceedings and a transcript of the evidence taken at the hearings, certified under the hands of at least a majority of the arbitrators, to the clerk of the district court of the United States for the district wherein the controversy arose or the arbitration is entered into, to be filed in said clerk's office as hereinafter provided. The said board shall also furnish a certified copy of its award, and the papers and proceedings, including testimony relating thereto, to the Mediation Board to be filed in its office; and in addition a certified copy of its award shall be filed in the office of the Interstate Commerce Commission: *Provided, however,* That such award shall not be construed to diminish or extinguish any of the powers or duties of the Interstate Commerce Commission, under the Interstate Commerce Act, as amended.

### (g) Compensation of assistants to board of arbitration; expenses; quarters.

A board of arbitration may, subject to the approval of the Mediation Board, employ and fix the compensation of such assistants as it deems necessary in carrying on the abitration proceedings. The compensation of such employees, together with their necessary traveling expenses and expenses actually incurred for subsistence, while so employed, and the necessary expenses of boards of arbitration, shall be paid by the Mediation Board.

Whenever practicable, the board shall be supplied with suitable quarters in any Federal building located at its place of meeting or at any place where the board may conduct its proceedings or deliberations.

### (h) Testimony before board; oaths; attendance of witnesses; production of documents; subpoenas; compulsion of witnesses; fees.

All testimony before said board shall be given under oath or affirmation, and any member of the board shall have the power to administer oaths or affirmations. The board of arbitration, or any member thereof, shall have the power to require the attendance of witnesses and the production of such books, papers, contracts, agreements, and documents as may be deemed by the board of arbitration material to a just determination of the matters submitted to its arbitration, and may for that purpose request the clerk of the district court of the United States for the district wherein said arbitration is being conducted to issue the necessary subpoenas, and upon such request the said clerk or his duly authorized deputy shall be, and he is, authorized, and it shall be his duty, to issue such subpoenas.

Any witness appearing before a board of arbitration shall receive the same fees and mileage as witnesses in courts of the United States, to be paid by the party securing the subpoena.

### Sec. 8. Agreement to arbitrate; form and contents; signatures and acknowledgment; revocation.

The agreement to arbitrate—

(a) Shall be in writing;

(b) Shall stipulate that the arbitration is had under the provisions of this Act;

(c) Shall state whether the board of arbitration is to consist of three or of six members;

(d) Shall be signed by the duly accredited representatives of the carrier or carriers and the employees, parties respectively to the agreement to arbitrate, and shall be acknowledged by said parties before a notary public, the clerk of a district court or court of appeals of the United States, or before a member of the Mediation Board, and, when so acknowledged, shall be filed in the office of the Mediation Board;

(e) Shall state specifically the questions to be submitted to the said board for decision; and that, in its award or awards, the said board shall confine itself strictly to decisions as to the questions so specifically submitted to it;

(f) Shall provide that the questions, or any one or more of them, submitted by the parties to the board of arbitration may be withdrawn from arbitration on notice to that effect signed by the duly accredited representatives of all the parties and served on the board of arbitration;

(g) Shall stipulate that the signatures of a majority of said board of arbitration affixed to their award shall be competent to constitute a valid and binding award;

(h) Shall fix a period from the date of the appointment of the arbitrator or arbitrators necessary to complete the board (as provided for in the agreement) within which the said board shall commence its hearings;

(i) Shall fix a period from the beginning of the hearings within which the said board shall make and file its award: *Provided,* That the parties may agree at any time upon an extension of this period;

(j) Shall provide for the date from which the award shall become effective and shall fix the period during which the award shall continue in force;

(k) Shall provide that the award of the board of arbitration and the evidence of the proceedings before the board relating thereto, when certified under the hands of at least a majority of the arbitrators, shall be filed in the clerk's office of the district court of the United States for the district wherein the controversy arose or the arbitration was entered into, which district shall be designated in the agreement; and, when so filed, such award and proceedings shall constitute the full and complete record of the arbitration;

(*l*) Shall provide that the award, when so filed, shall be final and conclusive upon the parties as to the facts determined by said award and as to the merits of the controversy decided;

(m) Shall provide that any difference arising as to the meaning, or the application of the provisions, of an award made by a board of arbitration shall be referred back for a ruling to the same board, or, by agreement, to a subcommittee of such board; and that such ruling, when acknowledged in the same manner, and filed in the same district court clerk's office, as the original award, shall be a part of and shall have the same force and effect as such original award; and

(n) Shall provide that the respective parties to the award will each faithfully execute the same.

The said agreement to arbitrate, when properly signed and acknowledged as herein provided, shall not be revoked by a party to such agreement: *Provided, however,* That such agreement to arbitrate may at any time be revoked and canceled by the written agreement of both parties, signed by their duly accredited representatives, and (if no board of arbitration has yet been constituted under the agreement) delivered to the Mediation Board or any member thereof; or, if the board of arbitration has been constituted as provided by this Act, delivered to such board of arbitration.

### Sec. 9.  Award and judgment thereon;  effect of Act on individual employee.

### First.  Filing of award.

The award of a board of arbitration, having been acknowledged as herein provided, shall be filed in the clerk's office of the district court designated in the agreement to arbitrate.

### Second.  Conclusiveness of award;  judgment.

An award acknowledged and filed as herein provided shall be conclusive on the parties as to the merits and facts of the controversy submitted to arbitration, and unless, within ten days after the filing of the award, a petition to impeach the award, on the grounds hereinafter set forth, shall be filed in the clerk's office of the court in which the award has been filed, the court shall enter judgment on the award, which judgment shall be final and conclusive on the parties.

### Third.  Impeachment of award;  grounds.

Such petition for the impeachment or contesting of any award so filed shall be entertained by the court only on one or more of the following grounds:

(a) That the award plainly does not conform to the substantive requirements laid down by this Act for such awards, or that the proceedings were not substantially in conformity with this Act;

(b) That the award does not conform, nor confine itself, to the stipulations of the agreement to arbitrate;  or

(c) That a member of the board of arbitration rendering the award was guilty of fraud or corruption;  or that a party to the arbitration practiced fraud or corruption which fraud or corruption affected the result of the arbitration: *Provided, however,* That no court shall entertain any such petition on the ground that an award is invalid for uncertainty;  in such case the proper remedy shall be a submission of such award to a reconvened board, or subcommittee thereof, for interpretation, as provided by this Act: *Provided further,* That an award contested as herein provided shall be construed liberally by the court, with a view to favoring its validity, and that no award shall be set aside for trivial irregularity or clerical error, going only to form and not to substance.

### Fourth.   Effect of partial invalidity of award.

If the court shall determine that a part of the award is invalid on some ground or grounds designated in this section as a ground of invalidity, but shall determine that a part of the award is valid, the court shall set aside the entire award: *Provided, however,* That, if the parties shall agree thereto, and if such valid and invalid parts are separable, the court shall set aside the invalid part, and order judgment to stand as to the valid part.

### Fifth.   Appeal; record.

At the expiration of 10 days from the decision of the district court upon the petition filed as aforesaid, final judgment shall be entered in accordance with said decision, unless during said 10 days either party shall appeal therefrom to the court of appeals. In such case only such portion of the record shall be transmitted to the appellate court as is necessary to the proper understanding and consideration of the questions of law presented by said petition and to be decided.

### Sixth.   Finality of decision of court of appeals.

The determination of said court of appeals upon said questions shall be final, and, being certified by the clerk thereof to said district court, judgment pursuant thereto shall thereupon be entered by said district court.

### Seventh.   Judgment where petitioner's contentions are sustained.

If the petitioner's contentions are finally sustained, judgment shall be entered setting aside the award in whole or, if the parties so agree, in part; but in such case the parties may agree upon a judgment to be entered disposing of the subject matter of the controversy, which judgment when entered shall have the same force and effect as judgment entered upon an award.

### Eighth.   Duty of employee to render service without consent; right to quit.

Nothing in this Act shall be construed to require an individual employee to render labor or service without his consent, nor shall anything in this Act be construed to make the quitting of his labor or service by an individual employee an illegal act; nor shall any court issue any process to compel the performance by an individual employee of such labor or service, without his consent.

## Sec. 9A. Special procedure for commuter service.

(a) Except as provided in section 510(h) of the Rail Passenger Service Act, the provisions of this section shall apply to any dispute subject to this Act between a publicly funded and publicly operated carrier providing rail commuter service (including the Amtrak Commuter Services Corporation) and its employees.

(b) If a dispute between the parties described in subsection (a) is not adjusted under the foregoing provisions of this Act and the President does not, under section 10 of this Act, create an emergency board to investigate and report on such dispute, then any party to the dispute or the Governor of any State through which the service that is the subject of the dispute is operated may request the President to establish such an emergency board.

(c)(1) Upon the request of a party or a Governor under subsection (b), the President shall create an emergency board to investigate and report on the dispute in accordance with section 10 of this Act. For purposes of this subsection, the period during which no change, except by agreement, shall be made by the parties in the conditions out of which the dispute arose shall be 120 days from the date of the creation of such emergency board.

(2) If the President, in his discretion, creates a board to investigate and report on a dispute between the parties described in subsection (a), the provisions of this section shall apply to the same extent as if such board had been created pursuant to paragraph (1) of this subsection.

(d) Within 60 days after the creation of an emergency board under this section, if there has been no settlement between the parties, the National Mediation Board shall conduct a public hearing on the dispute at which each party shall appear and provide testimony setting forth the reasons it has not accepted the recommendations of the emergency board for settlement of the dispute.

(e) If no settlement in the dispute is reached at the end of the 120-day period beginning on the date of the creation of the emergency board, any party to the dispute or the Governor of any State through which the service that is the subject of the dispute is operated may request the President to establish another emergency board, in which case the President shall establish such emergency board.

(f) Within 30 days after creation of a board under subsection (e), the parties to the dispute shall submit to the board final offers for settlement of the dispute.

(g) Within 30 days after the submission of final offers under subsection (f), the emergency board shall submit a report to the President setting forth its selection of the most reasonable offer.

(h) From the time a request to establish a board is made under subsection (e) until 60 days after such board makes its report under subsection (g), no change, except by agreement, shall be made by the parties in the conditions out of which the dispute arose.

(i) If the emergency board selects the final offer submitted by the carrier and, after the expiration of the 60-day period described in subsection (h), the employees of such carrier engage in any work stoppage arising out of the dispute, such employees shall not be eligible during the period of such work stoppage for benefits under the Railroad Unemployment Insurance Act.

(j) If the emergency board selects the final offer submitted by the employees and, after the expiration of the 60-day period described in subsection (h), the carrier refuses to accept the final offer submitted by the employees and the employees of such carrier engage in any work stoppage arising out of the dispute, the carrier shall not participate in any benefits of any agreement between carriers which is designed to provide benefits to such carriers during a work stoppage.*

## Sec. 10.  Emergency Board.

If a dispute between a carrier and its employees be not adjusted under the foregoing provisions of this Act and should, in the judgment of the Mediation Board, threaten substantially to interrupt interstate commerce to a degree such as to deprive any section of the country of essential transportation service, the Mediation Board shall notify the President, who may thereupon, in his discretion, create a board to investigate and report respecting such dispute. Such board shall be composed of such number of persons as to the President may seem desirable: *Provided, however,* That no member appointed shall be pecuniarily or otherwise interested in any organization of employees or any carrier. The compensation of the members of any such board shall be fixed by the President. Such board shall be created separately in each instance and it shall investigate promptly the facts as to the dispute and make a report thereon to the President within thirty days from the date of its creation.

There is hereby authorized to be appropriated such sums as may be necessary for the expenses of such board, including the compensation and the necessary traveling expenses and expenses actually incurred for subsistence, of the members of the board. All expenditures of the board shall be allowed and paid on the presentation of itemized vouchers therefor approved by the chairman.

After the creation of such board and for thirty days after such board has made its report to the President, no change, except by agreement, shall be made by the parties to the controversy in the conditions out of which the dispute arose.

## Sec. 11.  Effect of partial invalidity of Act.

If any section, subsection, sentence, clause, or phrase of this Act is for any reason held to be unconstitutional, such decision shall

* Section 9A was enacted by Pub.L. No.
97–35, § 1157, 95 Stat. 681 (1981).

not affect the validity of the remaining portions of this Act.  All Acts or parts of Acts inconsistent with the provisions of this Act are repealed.

## TITLE II

### CARRIERS BY AIR

### Sec. 201.   Application of title I to carriers by air.

All of the provisions of title I of this Act except section 3 are extended to and shall cover every common carrier by air engaged in interstate or foreign commerce, and every carrier by air transporting mail for or under contract with the United States Government, and every air pilot or other person who performs any work as an employee or subordinate official of such carrier or carriers, subject to its or their continuing authority to supervise and direct the manner of rendition of his service.

### Sec. 202.   Same; duties, penalties, benefits, and privileges.

The duties, requirements, penalties, benefits, and privileges prescribed and established by the provisions of title I of this Act, except section 3, shall apply to said carriers by air and their employees in the same manner and to the same extent as though such carriers and their employees were specifically included within the definition of "carrier" and "employee", respectively, in section 1 thereof.

### Sec. 203.   Disputes within jurisdiction of Mediation Board.

The parties or either party to a dispute between an employee or a group of employees and a carrier or carriers by air may invoke the services of the National Mediation Board and the jurisdiction of said Mediation Board is extended to any of the following cases:

(a)  A dispute concerning changes in rates of pay, rules, or working conditions not adjusted by the parties in conference.

(b)  Any other dispute not referable to an adjustment board, as hereinafter provided, and not adjusted in conference between the parties, or where conferences are refused.

The National Mediation Board may proffer its services in case any labor emergency is found by it to exist at any time.

The services of the Mediation Board may be invoked in a case under this title in the same manner and to the same extent as are the disputes covered by section 5 of title I of this Act.

### Sec. 204.   System, group, or regional boards of adjustment.

The disputes between an employee or group of employees and a carrier or carriers by air growing out of grievances, or out of the interpretation or application of agreements concerning rates of pay, rules, or working conditions, including cases pending and unadjusted on the date of approval of this Act [April 10, 1936] before the National Labor Relations Board, shall be handled in the usual manner up to and including the chief operating officer of the carrier designated to handle such disputes; but, failing to reach an adjustment in this manner, the disputes may be referred by petition of the parties or by either party to an appropriate adjustment board, as hereinafter provided, with a full statement of the facts and supporting data bearing upon the disputes.

It shall be the duty of every carrier and of its employees, acting through their representatives, selected in accordance with the provisions of this title, to establish a board of adjustment of jurisdiction not exceeding the jurisdiction which may be lawfully exercised by system, group, or regional boards of adjustment, under the authority of section 3, title I, of this Act.

Such boards of adjustment may be established by agreement between employees and carriers either on any individual carrier, or system, or group of carriers by air and any class or classes of its or their employees; or pending the establishment of a permanent National Board of Adjustment as hereinafter provided. Nothing in this Act shall prevent said carriers by air, or any class or classes of their employees, both acting through their representatives selected in accordance with provisions of this title, from mutually agreeing to the establishment of a National Board of Adjustment of temporary duration and of similarly limited jurisdiction.

### Sec. 205. National Air Transport Adjustment Board.

When, in the judgment of the National Mediation Board, it shall be necessary to have a permanent national board of adjustment in order to provide for the prompt and orderly settlement of disputes between said carriers by air, or any of them, and its or their employees, growing out of grievances or out of the interpretation or application of agreements between said carriers by air or any of them, and any class or classes of its or their employees, covering rates of pay, rules, or working conditions, the National Mediation Board is empowered and directed, by its order duly made, published, and served, to direct the said carriers by air and such labor organizations of their employees, national in scope, as have been or may be recognized in accordance with the provisions of this Act, to select and designate four representatives who shall constitute a board which shall be known as the "National Air Transport Adjustment Board." Two members of said National Air Transport Adjustment Board shall be selected by said carriers by air and two members by the said labor organizations of the employees, within thirty days after the date of the order of the National Mediation Board, in the manner and by the procedure prescribed by section 3, title I of this Act for the selection and designation of members of the National Railroad Adjustment Board. The National Air Transport Adjustment Board shall meet within forty days after the date of the order of the National Mediation Board directing the selection and designation of its members and shall organize and adopt rules for conducting its proceedings, in the manner prescribed in section 3, title I, of this Act. Vacancies in membership or office shall be filled, members shall be appointed in case of failure of the carriers or of labor organizations of the employees to select and designate representatives, members of the National Air Transport Adjustment Board shall be compensated, hearings shall be held, findings and awards made, stated, served, and enforced, and the number and compensation of any necessary assistants shall be determined and the compensation of such employees shall be paid, all in the same manner and to the same extent as provided with reference to the National Railroad Adjustment Board by section 3, title I, of this Act. The powers and duties prescribed and established by the provisions of section 3, title I, of this Act with reference to the National Railroad Adjustment Board and the several divisions thereof are conferred upon and shall be exercised and performed in like manner and to the same extent by the said National Air Transport Adjustment Board, not exceeding, however, the jurisdiction conferred upon said National Air Transport Adjustment Board by the provisions of title II of this Act. From and after the organization of the National Air Transport Adjustment Board, if any system, group, or regional board of adjustment established by any carrier or carriers by air and any class or classes of its or their employees is not satisfactory to either party thereto, the said party, upon ninety days' notice to the other party, may elect to come under the jurisdiction of the National Air Transport Adjustment Board.

**Sec. 206. Pending cases before Labor Relations Board transferred to Mediation Board. [Omitted]**

**Sec. 207. Separability of provisions.**

If any provision of title II or application thereof to any person or circumstance is held invalid, the remainder of the title and the application of such provision to other persons or circumstances shall not be affected thereby.

# NATIONAL LABOR RELATIONS ACT *

49 Stat. 449 (1935), as amended by 61 Stat. 136 (1947), 65 Stat. 601 (1951),
72 Stat. 945 (1958), 73 Stat. 541 (1959);
29 U.S.C. §§ 151–68 (1982).

## FINDINGS AND POLICIES

**Sec. 1.** The denial by *some* employers of the right of employees to organize and the refusal by *some* employers to accept the procedure of collective bargaining lead to strikes and other forms of industrial strife or unrest, which have the intent or the necessary effect of burdening or obstructing commerce by (a) impairing the efficiency, safety, or operation of the instrumentalities of commerce; (b) occurring in the current of commerce; (c) materially affecting, restraining, or controlling the flow of raw materials or manufactured or processed goods from or into the channels of commerce, or the prices of such materials or goods in commerce; or (d) causing diminution of employment and wages in such volume as substantially to impair or disrupt the market for goods flowing from or into the channels of commerce.

The inequality of bargaining power between employees who do not possess full freedom of association or actual liberty of contract, and employers who are organized in the corporate or other forms of ownership association substantially burdens and affects the flow of commerce, and tends to aggravate recurrent business depressions, by depressing wage rates and the purchasing power of wage earners in industry and by preventing the stabilization of competitive wage rates and working conditions within and between industries.

Experience has proved that protection by law of the right of employees to organize and bargain collectively safeguards commerce from injury, impairment, or interruption, and promotes the flow of commerce by removing certain recognized sources of industrial strife and unrest, by encouraging practices fundamental to the friendly adjustment of industrial disputes arising out of differences as to wages, hours, or other working conditions, and by restoring equality of bargaining power between employers and employees.

*Experience has further demonstrated that certain practices by some labor organizations, their officers, and members have the intent or the necessary effect of burdening or obstructing commerce by pre-*

---

* Language from the Wagner Act of 1935 is in roman type; language from the Taft-Hartley amendments of 1947 is in italics; language from the Landrum-Griffin amendments of 1959 is underscored. Deleted matter is in brackets; bracketed matter in roman type was deleted in 1947, bracketed matter in italics in 1959.

In 1974 the Act was amended to include health care institutions within its coverage. Pub.L. No. 93–360, 88 Stat. 395 (1974). Language from the 1974 legislation is in bold; bracketed matter in bold type was deleted in 1974.

*venting the free flow of goods in such commerce through strikes and other forms of industrial unrest or through concerted activities which impair the interest of the public in the free flow of such commerce. The elimination of such practices is a necessary condition to the assurance of the rights herein guaranteed.*

It is hereby declared to be the policy of the United States to eliminate the causes of certain substantial obstructions to the free flow of commerce and to mitigate and eliminate these obstructions when they have occurred by encouraging the practice and procedure of collective bargaining and by protecting the exercise by workers of full freedom of association, self-organization, and designation of representatives of their own choosing, for the purpose of negotiating the terms and conditions of their employment or other mutual aid or protection.

## DEFINITIONS

**Sec. 2.** When used in this Act—

(1) The term "person" includes one or more individuals, *labor organizations,* partnerships, associations, corporations, legal representatives, trustees, trustees in cases under title 11 of the United States Code, or receivers.

(2) The term "employer" includes any person acting [in the interest] *as an agent* of an employer, directly or indirectly, but shall not include the United States *or any wholly owned Government corporation, or any Federal Reserve Bank,* or any State or political subdivision thereof, [**or any corporation or association operating a hospital, if no part of the net earnings inures to the benefit of any private shareholder or individual,**] or any person subject to the Railway Labor Act, as amended from time to time, or any labor organization (other than when acting as an employer), or anyone acting in the capacity of officer or agent of such labor organization.

(3) The term "employee" shall include any employee, and shall not be limited to the employees of a particular employer, unless the Act explicitly states otherwise, and shall include any individual whose work has ceased as a consequence of, or in connection with, any current labor dispute or because of any unfair labor practice, and who has not obtained any other regular and substantially equivalent employment, but shall not include any individual employed as an agricultural laborer, or in the domestic service of any family or person at his home, or any individual employed by his parent or spouse, *or any individual having the status of an independent contractor, or any individual employed as a supervisor, or any individual employed by an employer subject to the Railway Labor Act, as amended from time to time, or by any other person who is not an employer as herein defined.*

(4) The term "representatives" includes any individual or labor organization.

(5) The term "labor organization" means any organization of any kind, or any agency or employee representation committee or plan, in which employees participate and which exists for the purpose, in whole or in part, of dealing with employers concerning grievances, labor disputes, wages, rates of pay, hours of employment, or conditions of work.

(6) The term "commerce" means trade, traffic, commerce, transportation, or communication among the several States, or between the District of Columbia or any Territory of the United States and any State or other Territory, or between any foreign country and any State, Territory, or the District of Columbia, or within the District of Columbia or any Territory, or between points in the same State but through any other State or any Territory or the District of Columbia or any foreign country.

(7) The term "affecting commerce" means in commerce, or burdening or obstructing commerce or the free flow of commerce, or having led or tending to lead to a labor dispute burdening or obstructing commerce or the free flow of commerce.

(8) The term "unfair labor practice" means any unfair labor practice listed in section 8.

(9) The term "labor dispute" includes any controversy concerning terms, tenure or conditions of employment, or concerning the association or representation of persons in negotiating, fixing, maintaining, changing, or seeking to arrange terms or conditions of employment, regardless of whether the disputants stand in the proximate relation of employer and employee.

(10) The term "National Labor Relations Board" means the National Labor Relations Board provided for in section 3 of this Act.

*(11) The term "supervisor" means any individual having authority, in the interest of the employer, to hire, transfer, suspend, lay off, recall, promote, discharge, assign, reward, or discipline other employees, or responsibly to direct them, or to adjust their grievances, or effectively to recommend such action, if in connection with the foregoing the exercise of such authority is not of a merely routine or clerical nature, but requires the use of independent judgment.*

*(12) The term "professional employee" means—*

*(a) any employee engaged in work (i) predominantly intellectual and varied in character as opposed to routine mental, manual, mechanical, or physical work; (ii) involving the consistent exercise of discretion and judgment in its performance; (iii) of such a character that the output pro-*

*duced or the result accomplished cannot be standardized in relation to a given period of time; (iv) requiring knowledge of an advanced type in a field of science or learning customarily acquired by a prolonged course of specialized intellectual instruction and study in an institution of higher learning or a hospital, as distinguished from a general academic education or from an apprenticeship or from training in the performance of routine mental, manual, or physical processes; or*

*(b) any employee, who (i) has completed the courses of specialized intellectual instruction and study described in clause (iv) of paragraph (a), and (ii) is performing related work under the supervision of a professional person to qualify himself to become a professional employee as defined in paragraph (a).*

*(13) In determining whether any person is acting as an "agent" of another person so as to make such other person responsible for his acts, the question of whether the specific acts performed were actually authorized or subsequently ratified shall not be controlling.*

**(14) The term "health care institution" shall include any hospital, canvalescent hospital, health maintenance organization, health clinic, nursing home, extended care facility, or other institution devoted to the care of sick, infirm, or aged persons.**

## NATIONAL LABOR RELATIONS BOARD

**Sec. 3.** (a) *The National Labor Relations Board (hereinafter called the "Board") created by this Act prior to its amendment by the Labor Management Relations Act, 1947, is hereby continued as an agency of the United States, except that the Board shall consist of five instead of three members, appointed by the President by and with the advice and consent of the Senate. Of the two additional members so provided for, one shall be appointed for a term of five years and the other for a term of two years. Their successors, and the successors of the other members, shall be appointed for terms of five years each, excepting that any individual chosen to fill a vacancy shall be appointed only for the unexpired term of the member whom he shall succeed. The President shall designate one member to serve as Chairman of the Board. Any member of the Board may be removed by the President, upon notice and hearing, for neglect of duty or malfeasance in office, but for no other cause.*

*(b) The Board is authorized to delegate to any group of three or more members any or all of the powers which it may itself exercise.* The Board is also authorized to delegate to its regional directors its powers under section 9 to determine the unit appropriate for the pur-

pose of collective bargaining, to investigate and provide for hearings, and determine whether a question of representation exists, and to direct an election or take a secret ballot under subsection (c) or (e) of section 9 and certify the results thereof, except that upon the filing of a request therefor with the Board by any interested person, the Board may review any action of a regional director delegated to him under this paragraph, but such a review shall not, unless specifically ordered by the Board, operate as a stay of any action taken by the regional director. *A vacancy in the Board shall not impair the right of the remaining members to exercise all of the powers of the Board, and three members of the Board shall, at all times, constitute a quorum of the Board, except that two members shall constitute a quorum of any group designated pursuant to the first sentence hereof. The Board shall have an official seal which shall be judicially noticed.*

(c) The Board shall at the close of each fiscal year make a report in writing to Congress and to the President [stating in detail the cases it has heard, the decisions it has rendered, the names, salaries, and duties of all employees and officers in the employ or under the supervision of the Board, and an account of all moneys it has disbursed] * summarizing significant case activities and operations for that fiscal year.

*(d) There shall be a General Counsel of the Board who shall be appointed by the President, by and with the advice and consent of the Senate, for a term of four years. The General Counsel of the Board shall exercise general supervision over all attorneys employed by the Board (other than trial examiners and legal assistants to Board members) and over the officers and employees in the regional offices. He shall have final authority, on behalf of the Board, in respect of the investigation of charges and issuance of complaints under section 10, and in respect of the prosecution of such complaints before the Board, and shall have such other duties as the Board may prescribe or as may be provided by law.* In case of a vacancy in the office of the General Counsel the President is authorized to designate the officer or employee who shall act as General Counsel during such vacancy, but no person or persons so designated shall so act (1) for more than forty days when the Congress is in session unless a nomination to fill such vacancy shall have been submitted to the Senate, or (2) after the adjournment sine die of the session of the Senate in which such nomination was submitted.**

**Sec. 4.\*\*** *(a) Each member of the Board and the General Counsel of the Board shall receive a salary of $12,000* *** *a year, shall be*

---

* This bracketed matter was deleted by Pub.L. No. 93–608 (1975), Pub.L. No. 97–375 (1982).

** The changes made in Sections 3 and 4 of the National Labor Relations Act by the Taft-Hartley amendments of 1947 were too extensive to be indicated by italicizing new matter *and* bracketing deletions. The sections are reproduced here as amended in 1947 and again in 1959.

*** The salaries of Board members and of the General Counsel are now pre-

*eligible for reappointment, and shall not engage in any other busi-
ness, vocation, or employment.* The Board shall appoint an executive
secretary, and such attorneys, examiners, and regional directors, and
such other employees as it may from time to time find necessary for
the proper performance of its duties. The Board may not employ
any attorneys for the purpose of reviewing transcripts of hearings or
preparing drafts of opinions except that any attorney employed for
assignment as a legal assistant to any Board member may for such
Board member review such transcripts and prepare such drafts. No
trial examiner's report shall be reviewed, either before or after its
publication, by any person other than a member of the Board or his
legal assistant, and no trial examiner shall advise or consult with the
Board with respect to exceptions taken to his findings, rulings, or
recommendations. The Board may establish or utilize such regional,
local, or other agencies, and utilize such voluntary and uncompensat-
ed services, as may from time to time be needed. Attorneys appointed
under this section may, at the direction of the Board, appear for and
represent the Board in any case in court. Nothing in this Act shall
be construed to authorize the Board to appoint individuals for the
purpose of conciliation or mediation, or for economic analysis.*

*(b) All of the expenses of the Board, including all necessary
traveling and subsistence expenses outside the District of Columbia
incurred by the members or employees of the Board under its orders,
shall be allowed and paid on the presentation of itemized vouchers
therefor approved by the Board or by any individual it designates for
that purpose.*

**Sec. 5.** The principal office of the Board shall be in the District
of Columbia, but it may meet and exercise any or all of its powers at
any other place. The Board may, by one or more of its members or
by such agents or agencies as it may designate, prosecute any inquiry necessary to its functions in any part of the United States. A
member who participates in such an inquiry shall not be disqualified
from subsequently participating in a decision of the Board in the
same case.

**Sec. 6.** The Board shall have authority from time to time to
make, amend, and rescind, *in the manner prescribed by the Administrative Procedure Act,* such rules and regulations as may be necessary
to carry out the provisions of this Act. [Such rules and regulations
shall be effective upon publication in the manner which the Board
shall prescribe.]

scribed in the Federal Executive Salary
Schedule. As of January 1, 1984, the
salary of the Board Chairman became
$70,800 per year and that of the other
Board members and the General Counsel
$69,600 per year. See 5 U.S.C.A. §§
5314, 5315 (and notes following) (West
Supp. 1985).

## RIGHTS OF EMPLOYEES

**Sec. 7.** Employees shall have the right to self-organization, to form, join, or assist labor organizations, to bargain collectively through representatives of their own choosing, and to engage in *other* concerted activities for the purpose of collective bargaining or other mutual aid or protection, *and shall also have the right to refrain from any or all of such activities except to the extent that such right may be affected by an agreement requiring membership in a labor organization as a condition of employment as authorized in section 8(a) (3).*

## UNFAIR LABOR PRACTICES

**Sec. 8.** (a) It shall be an unfair labor practice for an employer—

(1) to interfere with, restrain, or coerce employees in the exercise of the rights guaranteed in section 7;

(2) to dominate or interfere with the formation or administration of any labor organization or contribute financial or other support to it: *Provided,* That subject to rules and regulations made and published by the Board pursuant to section 6, an employer shall not be prohibited from permitting employees to confer with him during working hours without loss of time or pay;

(3) by discrimination in regard to hire or tenure of employment or any term or condition of employment to encourage or discourage membership in any labor organization: *Provided,* That nothing in this Act, or in any other statute of the United States, shall preclude an employer from making an agreement with a labor organization (not established, maintained, or assisted by any action defined in *section 8(a) of* this Act as an unfair labor practice) to require as a condition of employment membership therein *on or after the thirtieth day following the beginning of such employment or the effective date of such agreement, whichever is the later, (i)* if such labor organization is the representative of the employees as provided in section 9(a), in the appropriate collective-bargaining unit covered by such agreement when made;  [*and has at the time the agreement was made or within the preceding twelve months received from the Board a notice of compliance with section 9(f), (g), (h)*] *and (ii) unless following an election held as provided in section 9(e) within one year preceding the effective date of such agreement, the Board shall have certified that at least a majority of the employees eligible to vote in such election have voted to rescind the authority of such labor organization to make such an agreement:* * *Provided further, That no employer shall justify any*

---

* The (ii) provision was added in 1951
by 65 Stat. 601.

*discrimination against an employee for non-membership in a labor organization (A) if he has reasonable grounds for believing that such membership was not available to the employee on the same terms and conditions generally applicable to other members, or (B) if he has reasonable grounds for believing that membership was denied or terminated for reasons other than the failure of the employee to tender the periodic dues and the initiation fees uniformly required as a condition of acquiring or retaining membership;*

(4) to discharge or otherwise discriminate against an employee because he has filed charges or given testimony under this Act;

(5) to refuse to bargain collectively with the representatives of his employees, subject to the provisions of section 9(a).

*(b) It shall be an unfair labor practice for a labor organization or its agents—*

*(1) to restrain or coerce (A) employees in the exercise of the rights guaranteed in section 7: Provided, That this paragraph shall not impair the right of a labor organization to prescribe its own rules with respect to the acquisition or retention of membership therein; or (B) an employer in the selection of his representatives for the purposes of collective bargaining or the adjustment of grievances;*

*(2) to cause or attempt to cause an employer to discriminate against an employee in violation of subsection (a) (3) or to discriminate against an employee with respect to whom membership in such organization has been denied or terminated on some ground other than his failure to tender the periodic dues and the initiation fees uniformly required as a condition of acquiring or retaining membership;*

*(3) to refuse to bargain collectively with an employer, provided it is the representative of his employees subject to the provisions of section 9(a);*

*(4)* (i) *to engage in, or to induce or encourage [the employees of any employer]* any individual employed by any person engaged in commerce or in an industry affecting commerce *to engage in, a strike or a [concerted]* refusal in the course of [their] his *employment to use, manufacture, process, transport, or otherwise handle or work on any goods, articles, materials, or commodities or to perform any services;* or (ii) to threaten, coerce, or restrain any person engaged in commerce or in an industry affecting commerce, *where* in either case *an object thereof is—*

*(A) forcing or requiring any employer or self-employed person to join any labor or employer organization or [any employer or other person to cease using, selling, handling, trans-*

porting, or otherwise dealing in the products of any other producer, processor, or manufacturer, or to cease doing business with any other person] to enter into any agreement which is prohibited by section 8(e);

(B) forcing or requiring any person to cease using, selling, handling, transporting, or otherwise dealing in the products of any other producer, processor, or manufacturer, or to cease doing business with any other person, or *forcing or requiring any other employer to recognize or bargain with a labor organization as the representative of his employees unless such labor organization has been certified as the representative of such employees under the provisions of section 9:* Provided, That nothing contained in this clause (B) shall be construed to make unlawful, where not otherwise unlawful, any primary strike or primary picketing;

*(C) forcing or requiring any employer to recognize or bargain with a particular labor organization as the representative of his employees if another labor organization has been certified as the representative of such employees under the provisions of section 9;*

*(D) forcing or requiring any employer to assign particular work to employees in a particular labor organization or in a particular trade, craft, or class rather than to employees in another labor organization or in another trade, craft, or class, unless such employer is failing to conform to an order or certification of the Board determining the bargaining representative for employees performing such work:*

*Provided, That nothing contained in this subsection (b) shall be construed to make unlawful a refusal by any person to enter upon the premises of any employer (other than his own employer), if the employees of such employer are engaged in a strike ratified or approved by a representative of such employees whom such employer is required to recognize under this Act:* Provided further, That for the purposes of this paragraph (4) only, nothing contained in such paragraph shall be construed to prohibit publicity, other than picketing, for the purpose of truthfully advising the public, including consumers and members of a labor organization, that a product or products are produced by an employer with whom the labor organization has a primary dispute and are distributed by another employer, as long as such publicity does not have an effect of inducing any individual employed by any person other than the primary employer in the course of his employment to refuse to pick up, deliver, or transport any goods, or not to perform any services, at the establishment of the employer engaged in such distribution;

*(5) to require of employees covered by an agreement authorized under subsection (a) (3) the payment, as a condition precedent to becoming a member of such organization, of a fee in an amount which the Board finds excessive or discriminatory under all the circumstances. In making such a finding, the Board shall consider, among other relevant factors, the practices and customs of labor organizations in the particular industry, and the wages currently paid to the employees affected;* [*and*]

*(6) to cause or attempt to cause an employer to pay or deliver or agree to pay or deliver any money or other thing of value, in the nature of an exaction, for services which are not performed or not to be performed;* and

(7) to picket or cause to be picketed, or threaten to picket or cause to be picketed, any employer where an object thereof is forcing or requiring an employer to recognize or bargain with a labor organization as the representative of his employees, or forcing or requiring the employees of an employer to accept or select such labor organization as their collective bargaining representative, unless such labor organization is currently certified as the representative of such employees:

What is prohibited

(A) where the employer has lawfully recognized in accordance with this Act any other labor organization and a question concerning representation may not appropriately be raised under section 9(c) of this Act,

(B) where within the preceding twelve months a valid election under section 9(c) of this Act has been conducted, or

What Circumstanse

(C) where such picketing has been conducted without a petition under section 9(c) being filed within a reasonable period of time not to exceed thirty days from the commencement of such picketing: Provided, That when such a petition has been filed the Board shall forthwith, without regard to the provisions of section 9(c)(1) or the absence of a showing of a substantial interest on the part of the labor organization, direct an election in such unit as the Board finds to be appropriate and shall certify the results thereof: Provided further, That nothing in this subparagraph (C) shall be construed to prohibit any picketing or other publicity for the purpose of truthfully advising the public (including consumers) that an employer does not employ members of, or have a contract with, a labor organization, unless an effect of such picketing is to induce any individual employed by any other

Both must be present for violation to be

person in the course of his employment, not to pick up, deliver or transport any goods or not to perform any services.

Nothing in this paragraph (7) shall be construed to permit any act which would otherwise be an unfair labor practice under this section 8(b).

*(c) The expressing of any views, argument, or opinion, or the dissemination thereof, whether in written, printed, graphic, or visual form, shall not constitute or be evidence of an unfair labor practice under any of the provisions of this Act, if such expression contains no threat of reprisal or force or promise of benefit.*

*(d) For the purposes of this section, to bargain collectively is the performance of the mutual obligation of the employer and the representative of the employees to meet at reasonable times and confer in good faith with respect to wages, hours, and other terms and conditions of employment, or the negotiation of an agreement, or any question arising thereunder, and the execution of a written contract incorporating any agreement reached if requested by either party, but such obligation does not compel either party to agree to a proposal or require the making of a concession: Provided, That where there is in effect a collective-bargaining contract covering employees in an industry affecting commerce, the duty to bargain collectively shall also mean that no party to such contract shall terminate or modify such contract, unless the party desiring such termination or modification—*

*(1) serves a written notice upon the other party to the contract of the proposed termination or modification sixty days prior to the expiration date thereof, or in the event such contract contains no expiration date, sixty days prior to the time it is proposed to make such termination or modification;*

*(2) offers to meet and confer with the other party for the purpose of negotiating a new contract or a contract containing the proposed modifications;*

*(3) notifies the Federal Mediation and Conciliation Service within thirty days after such notice of the existence of a dispute, and simultaneously therewith notifies any State or Territorial agency established to mediate and conciliate disputes within the State or Territory where the dispute occurred, provided no agreement has been reached by that time; and*

*(4) continues in full force and effect, without resorting to strike or lockout, all the terms and conditions of the existing contract for a period of sixty days after such notice is given or until the expiration date of such contract, whichever occurs later:*

*The duties imposed upon employers, employees, and labor organizations by paragraphs (2), (3), and (4) shall become inapplicable upon an intervening certification of the Board, under which the labor or-ganization or individual, which is a party to the contract, has been superseded as or ceased to be the representative of the employees sub-ject to the provisions of section 9(a), and the duties so imposed shall not be construed as requiring either party to discuss or agree to any modification of the terms and conditions contained in a contract for a fixed period, if such modification is to become effective before such terms and conditions can be reopened under the provi-sions of the contract.* **Any employee who engages in a strike within [the sixty-day] any notice** *period specified in this subsection,* **or who engages in any strike within the appropriate period specified in sub-section (g) of this section,** *shall lose his status as an employee of the employer engaged in the particular labor dispute, for the purposes of sections 8, 9, and 10 of this Act, as amended, but such loss of status for such employee shall terminate if and when he is reemployed by such employer.* **Whenever the collective bargaining involves the em-ployees of a health care institution, the provisions of this section shall be modified as follows:**

> **(A) The notice of section 8(d)(1) shall be ninety days; the notice of section 8(d)(3) shall be sixty days; and the contract period of section 8(d)(4) shall be ninety days.**

> **(B) Where the bargaining is for an initial agreement follow-ing certification or recognition, at least thirty days' notice of the existence of a dispute shall be given by the labor organization to the agencies set forth in section 8(d)(3).**

> **(C) After notice is given to the Federal Mediation and Con-ciliation Service under either clause (A) or (B) of this sentence, the Service shall promptly communicate with the parties and use its best efforts by mediation and conciliation to bring them to agreement. The parties shall participate fully and promptly in such meetings as may be undertaken by the Service for the pur-pose of aiding in the settlement of the dispute.**

(e) It shall be an unfair labor practice for any labor organization and any employer to enter into any contract or agreement, express or implied, whereby such employer ceases or refrains or agrees to cease or refrain from handling, using, selling, transporting or other-wise dealing in any of the products of any other employer, or to cease doing business with any other person, and any contract or agreement entered into heretofore or hereafter containing such an agreement shall be to such extent unenforcible and void: Provided, That nothing in this subsection (e) shall apply to an agreement between a labor or-ganization and an employer in the construction industry relating to the contracting or subcontracting of work to be done at the site of the construction, alteration, painting, or repair of a building, structure, or other work: Provided further, That for the purposes of this subsection (e) and section 8(b)(4)(B) the terms "any employer", "any person engaged in commerce or an industry affecting commerce", and "any person" when used in relation to the terms "any other producer, processor, or manufacturer", "any other employer", or "any other person" shall not include persons in the relation of a jobber, manufacturer, contractor, or subcontractor working on the goods or premises of the jobber or manufacturer or performing parts of an integrated process of production in the apparel and clothing industry: Provided further, That nothing in this Act shall prohibit the enforcement of any agreement which is within the foregoing exception.

(f) It shall not be an unfair labor practice under subsections (a) and (b) of this section for an employer engaged primarily in the building and construction industry to make an agreement covering employees engaged (or who, upon their employment, will be engaged) in the building and construction industry with a labor organization of which building and construction employees are members (not established, maintained, or assisted by any action defined in section 8 (a) of this Act as an unfair labor practice) because (1) the majority status of such labor organization has not been established under the provisions of section 9 of this Act prior to the making of such agreement, or (2) such agreement requires as a condition of employment, membership in such labor organization after the seventh day following the beginning of such employment or the effective date of the agreement, whichever is later, or (3) such agreement requires the employer to notify such labor organization of opportunities for employment with such employer, or gives such labor organization an opportunity to refer qualified applicants for such employment, or (4) such agreement specifies minimum training or experience qualifications for employment or provides for priority in opportunities for employment based upon length of service with such employer, in the industry or in the particular geographical area: Provided, That nothing in this subsection shall set aside the final proviso to section 8(a)(3) of this Act: Provided further, That any agreement which would be invalid, but for clause (1) of this subsection, shall not be a bar to a petition filed pursuant to section 9(c) or 9(e).*

**(g) A labor organization before engaging in any strike, picketing, or other concerted refusal to work at any health care institution shall, not less than ten days prior to such action, notify the Federal Mediation and Conciliation Service of that intention, except that in the case of bargaining for an initial agreement following certification or rec-**

---

* Section 8(f) was added to the NLRA by Section 705(a) of the Landrum-Griffin amendments of 1959. Section 705 (b) provides:

"Nothing contained in the amendment made by subsection (a) shall be construed as authorizing the execution or application of agreements requiring membership in a labor organization as a condition of employment in any State or Territory in which such execution or application is prohibited by State or Territorial law."

ognition the notice required by this subsection shall not be given until the expiration of the period specified in clause (B) of the last sentence of section 8(d) of this Act. The notice shall state the date and time that such action will commence. The notice, once given, may be extended by the written agreement of both parties.

## REPRESENTATIVES AND ELECTIONS

**Sec. 9.** (a) Representatives designated or selected for the purposes of collective bargaining by the majority of the employees in a unit appropriate for such purposes, shall be the exclusive representatives of all the employees in such unit for the purposes of collective bargaining in respect to rates of pay, wages, hours of employment, or other conditions of employment: *Provided,* That any individual employee or a group of employees shall have the right at any time to present grievances to their employer *and to have such grievances adjusted, without the intervention of the bargaining representative, as long as the adjustment is not inconsistent with the terms of a collective-bargaining contract or agreement then in effect: Provided further, That the bargaining representative has been given opportunity to be present at such adjustment.*

(b) The Board shall decide in each case whether, in order to assure to employees the fullest freedom in exercising the rights guaranteed by this Act, the unit appropriate for the purposes of collective bargaining shall be the employer unit, craft unit, plant unit, or subdivision thereof: *Provided, That the Board shall not (1) decide that any unit is appropriate for such purposes if such unit includes both professional employees and employees who are not professional employees unless a majority of such professional employees vote for inclusion in such unit; or (2) decide that any craft unit is inappropriate for such purposes on the ground that a different unit has been established by a prior Board determination, unless a majority of the employees in the proposed craft unit vote against separate representation or (3) decide that any unit is appropriate for such purposes if it includes, together with other employees, any individual employed as a guard to enforce against employees and other persons rules to protect property of the employer or to protect the safety of persons on the employer's premises; but no labor organization shall be certified as the representative of employees in a bargaining unit of guards if such organization admits to membership, or is affiliated directly or indirectly with an organization which admits to membership, employees other than guards.*

[(c) Whenever a question affecting commerce arises concerning the representation of employees, the Board may investigate such controversy and certify to the parties, in writing, the name or names of the representatives that have been designated or selected. In any such investigation, the Board shall provide for an appropriate hearing upon due notice, either in conjunction with a proceeding under section 10 or otherwise, and may take a secret ballot of employees, or utilize any other suitable method to ascertain such representatives.]

*(c) (1) Whenever a petition shall have been filed, in accordance with such regulations as may be prescribed by the Board—*

> *(A) by an employee or group of employees or any individual or labor organization acting in their behalf alleging that a substantial number of employees (i) wish to be represented for collective bargaining and that their employer declines to recognize their representative as the representative defined in section 9(a), or (ii) assert that the individual or labor organization, which has been certified or is being currently recognized by their employer as the bargaining representative, is no longer a representative as defined in section 9(a); or*

> *(B) by an employer, alleging that one or more individuals or labor organizations have presented to him a claim to be recognized as the representative defined in section 9(a);*

*the Board shall investigate such petition and if it has reasonable cause to believe that a question of representation affecting commerce exists shall provide for an appropriate hearing upon due notice. Such hearing may be conducted by an officer or employee of the regional office, who shall not make any recommendations with respect thereto. If the Board finds upon the record of such hearing that such a question of representation exists, it shall direct an election by secret ballot and shall certify the results thereof.*

*(2) In determining whether or not a question of representation affecting commerce exists, the same regulations and rules of decision shall apply irrespective of the identity of the persons filing the petition or the kind of relief sought and in no case shall the Board deny a labor organization a place on the ballot by reason of an order with respect to such labor organization or its predecessor not issued in conformity with section 10(c).*

*(3) No election shall be directed in any bargaining unit or any subdivision within which, in the preceding twelve-month period, a valid election shall have been held.* Employees [on] engaged in an economic *strike who are not entitled to reinstatement shall [not] be eligible to vote* under such regulations as the Board shall find are consistent with the purposes and provisions of this Act in any election conducted within twelve months after the commencement of the strike. *In any election where none of the*

*choices on the ballot receives a majority, a run-off shall be conducted, the ballot providing for a selection between the two choices receiving the largest and second largest number of valid votes cast in the election.*

*(4) Nothing in this section shall be construed to prohibit the waiving of hearings by stipulation for the purpose of a consent election in conformity with regulations and rules of decision of the Board.*

*(5) In determining whether a unit is appropriate for the purposes specified in subsection (b) the extent to which the employees have organized shall not be controlling.*

(d) Whenever an order of the Board made pursuant to section 10(c) is based in whole or in part upon facts certified following an investigation pursuant to subsection (c) of this section and there is a petiton for the enforcement or review of such order, such certification and the record of such investigation shall be included in the transcript of the entire record required to be filed under section 10(e) or 10(f), and thereupon the decree of the court enforcing, modifying, or setting aside in whole or in part the order of the Board shall be made and entered upon the pleadings, testimony, and proceedings set forth in such transcript.

*(e) (1) Upon the filing with the Board, by 30 per centum or more of the employees in a bargaining unit covered by an agreement between their employer and a labor organization made pursuant to section 8(a) (3), of a petition alleging they desire that such authority be rescinded, the Board shall take a secret ballot of the employees in such unit and certify the results thereof to such labor organization and to the employer.*

*(2) No election shall be conducted pursuant to this subsection in any bargaining unit or any subdivision within which, in the preceding twelve-month period, a valid election shall have been held.\**

*[(f) No investigation shall be made by the Board of any question affecting commerce concerning the representation of employees, raised by a labor organization under subsection (c) of this section, and no complaint shall be issued pursuant to a charge made by a labor organization under subsection (b) of section 10, unless such labor organization and any national or international labor organization of which such labor organization is an affiliate or constituent unit (A) shall have prior thereto filed with the Secretary of Labor copies of its con-*

---

\* As enacted in 1947, Section 9(e) had three subsections. In 1951, the first subsection was deleted and the two remaining subsections were renumbered (1) and (2). 65 Stat. 601. The subsection which was deleted required, as a prerequisite to the seeking of a union-shop provision in a collective bargaining agreement, that the union win a Board-conducted election authorizing such attempt.

*stitution and bylaws and a report, in such form as the Secretary may prescribe, showing—*

*(1) the name of such labor organization and the address of its principal place of business;*

*(2) the names, titles, and compensation and allowances of its three principal officers and of any of its other officers or agents whose aggregate compensation and allowances for the preceding year exceeded $5,000, and the amount of the compensation and allowances paid to each such officer or agent during such year;*

*(3) the manner in which the officers and agents referred to in clause (2) were elected, appointed, or otherwise selected;*

*(4) the initiation fee or fees which new members are required to pay on becoming members of such labor organization;*

*(5) the regular dues or fees which members are required to pay in order to remain members in good standing of such labor organization;*

*(6) a detailed statement of, or reference to provisions of its constitution and bylaws showing the procedure followed with respect to, (a) qualification for or restrictions on membership, (b) election of officers and stewards, (c) calling of regular and special meetings, (d) levying of assessments, (e) imposition of fines, (f) authorization for bargaining demands, (g) ratification of contract terms, (h) authorization for strikes, (i) authorization for disbursement of union funds, (j) audit of union financial transactions, (k) participation in insurance or other benefit plans, and (l) expulsion of members and the grounds therefor;*

*and (B) can show that prior thereto it has—*

*(1) filed with the Secretary of Labor, in such form as the Secretary may prescribe, a report showing all of (a) its receipts of any kind and the sources of such receipts, (b) its total assets and liabilities as of the end of its last fiscal year, (c) the disbursements made by it during such fiscal year, including the purposes for which made; and*

*(2) furnished to all of the members of such labor organization copies of the financial report required by paragraph (1) hereof to be filed with the Secretary of Labor.]*

*[(g) It shall be the obligation of all labor organizations to file annually with the Secretary of Labor, in such form as the Secretary of Labor may prescribe, reports bringing up to date the information required to be supplied in the initial filing by subsection (f) (A) of this section, and to file with the Secretary of Labor and furnish to its members annually financial reports in the form and manner prescribed in subsection (f) (B). No labor organization shall be eligible for certification under this section as the representative of any employees, and*

*no complaint shall issue under section 10 with respect to a charge
filed by a labor organization unless it can show that it and any national or international labor organization of which it is an affiliate or
constituent unit has complied with its obligation under this subsection.]*

*[(h) No investigation shall be made by the Board of any question
affecting commerce concerning the representation of employees, raised
by a labor organization under subsection (c) of this section, and no
complaint shall be issued pursuant to a charge made by a labor organization under subsection (b) of section 10, unless there is on file with
the Board an affidavit executed contemporaneously or within the preceding twelve-month period by each officer of such labor organization
and the officers of any national or international labor organization of
which it is an affiliate or constituent unit that he is not a member of
the Communist Party or affiliated with such party, and that he does
not believe in, and is not a member of or supports any organization
that believes in or teaches, the overthrow of the United States Government by force or by any illegal or unconstitutional methods. The provisions of section 35A of the Criminal Code shall be applicable in respect to such affidavits.]*

### Prevention of Unfair Labor Practices

**Sec. 10.**    (a) The Board is empowered, as hereinafter provided,
to prevent any person from engaging in any unfair labor practice
(listed in section 8) affecting commerce.  This power shall not be
affected by any other means of adjustment or prevention that has been
or may be established by agreement, law, or otherwise: *Provided,
That the Board is empowered by agreement with any agency of any
State or Territory to cede to such agency jurisdiction over any cases
in any industry (other than mining, manufacturing, communications,
and transportation except where predominantly local in character)
even though such cases may involve labor disputes affecting commerce, unless the provision of the State or Territorial statute applicable to the determination of such cases by such agency is inconsistent
with the corresponding provision of this Act or has received a construction inconsistent therewith.*

(b) Whenever it is charged that any person has engaged in or is
engaging in any such unfair labor practice, the Board, or any agent
or agency designated by the Board for such purposes, shall have power to issue and cause to be served upon such person a complaint stating the charges in that respect, and containing a notice of hearing before the Board or a member thereof, or before a designated agent or
agency, at a place therein fixed, not less than five days after the serving of said complaint: *Provided, That no complaint shall issue based
upon any unfair labor practice occurring more than six months prior
to the filing of the charge with the Board and the service of a copy
thereof upon the person against whom such charge is made, unless the*

*person aggrieved thereby was prevented from filing such charge by reason of service in the armed forces, in which event the six-month period shall be computed from the day of his discharge.* Any such complaint may be amended by the member, agent, or agency conducting the hearing or the Board in its discretion at any time prior to the issuance of an order based thereon. The person so complained of shall have the right to file an answer to the original or amended complaint and to appear in person or otherwise and give testimony at the place and time fixed in the complaint. In the discretion of the member, agent, or agency conducting the hearing or the Board, any other person may be allowed to intervene in the said proceeding and to present testimony. [In any such proceeding the rules of evidence prevailing in courts of law or equity shall not be controlling.] *Any such proceeding shall, so far as practicable, be conducted in accordance with the rules of evidence applicable in the district courts of the United States under the rules of civil procedure for the district courts of the United States, adopted by the Supreme Court of the United States pursuant to section 2072 of title 28, United States Code.*

(c) The testimony taken by such member, agent, or agency or the Board shall be reduced to writing and filed with the Board. Thereafter, in its discretion, the Board upon notice may take further testimony or hear argument. If upon [all] *the preponderance of* the testimony taken the Board shall be of the opinion that any person named in the complaint has engaged in or is engaging in any such unfair labor practice, then the Board shall state its findings of fact and shall issue and cause to be served on such person an order requiring such person to cease and desist from such unfair labor practice, and to take such affirmative action including reinstatement of employees with or without back pay, as will effectuate the policies of this Act: *Provided, That where an order directs reinstatement of an employee, back pay may be required of the employer or labor organization, as the case may be, responsible for the discrimination suffered by him: And provided further, That in determining whether a complaint shall issue alleging a violation of section 8(a) (1) or section 8(a) (2), and in deciding such cases, the same regulations and rules of decision shall apply irrespective of whether or not the labor organization affected is affiliated with a labor organization national or international in scope.* Such order may further require such person to make reports from time to time showing the extent to which it has complied with the order. If upon [all] *the preponderance of* the testimony taken the Board shall not be of the opinion that the person named in the complaint has engaged in or is engaging in any such unfair labor practice, then the Board shall state its findings of fact and shall issue an order dismissing the said complaint. *No order of the Board shall require the reinstatement of any individual as an employee who has been suspended or discharged, or the payment to him of any back pay, if such individual was suspended or discharged for cause. In case the evidence is presented before a member of the Board, or before an exam-*

*iner or examiners thereof, such member, or such examiner or exam-iners, as the case may be, shall issue and cause to be served on the parties to the proceeding a proposed report, together with a recom-mended order, which shall be filed with the Board, and if no excep-tions are filed within twenty days after service thereof upon such par-ties, or within such further period as the Board may authorize, such recommended order shall become the order of the Board and become effective as therein prescribed.*

(d) Until *a transcript of* the record in a case shall have been filed in a court, as hereinafter provided, the Board may at any time, upon reasonable notice and in such manner as it shall deem proper, modify or set aside, in whole or in part, any finding or order made or issued by it.

(e) The Board shall have power to petition any court of appeals of the United States, or if all the courts of appeals to which applica-tion may be made are in vacation, any district court of the United States, within any circuit or district, respectively, wherein the unfair labor practice in question occurred or wherein such person resides or transacts business, for the enforcement of such order and for appro-priate temporary relief or restraining order, and shall file in the court the record in the proceedings, as provided in section 2112 of title 28, United States Code. Upon the filing of such petition, the court shall cause notice thereof to be served upon such person, and thereupon shall have jurisdiction of the proceeding and of the question deter-mined therein, and shall have power to grant such temporary relief or restraining order as it deems just and proper, and to make and en-ter a decree enforcing, modifying, and enforcing as so modified, or setting aside in whole or in part the order of the Board. No objec-tion that has not been urged before the Board, its member, agent, or agency, shall be considered by the court, unless the failure or neglect to urge such objection shall be excused because of extraordinary cir-cumstances. The findings of the Board with respect to questions of fact if supported by *substantial* evidence *on the record considered as a whole* shall be conclusive. If either party shall apply to the court for leave to adduce additional evidence and shall show to the satis-faction of the court that such additional evidence is material and that there were reasonable grounds for the failure to adduce such evidence in the hearing before the Board, its member, agent, or agency, the court may order such additional evidence to be taken before the Board, its member, agent, or agency, and to be made a part of the record. The Board may modify its findings as to the facts, or make new find-ings, by reason of additional evidence so taken and filed, and it shall file such modified or new findings, which findings with respect to questions of fact if supported by *substantial* evidence *on the record considered as a whole* shall be conclusive, and shall file its recom-mendations, if any, for the modification or setting aside of its original order. Upon the filing of the record with it the jurisdiction of the court shall be exclusive and its judgment and decree shall be final, except that the same shall be subject to review by the appropriate United States court of appeals if application was made to the district court as hereinabove provided, and by the Supreme Court of the United States upon writ of certiorari or certification as provided in section 1254 of title 28.

(f) Any person aggrieved by a final order of the Board granting or denying in whole or in part the relief sought may obtain a review of such order in any circuit court of appeals of the United States in the circuit wherein the unfair labor practice in question was alleged to have been engaged in or wherein such person resides or transacts business, or in the United States Court of Appeals for the District of Columbia, by filing in such court a written petition praying that the order of the Board be modified or set aside. A copy of such petition shall be forthwith transmitted by the clerk of the court to the Board, and thereupon the aggrieved party shall file in the court the record in the proceeding, certified by the Board, as provided in section 2112 of title 28, United States Code. Upon the filing of such petition, the court shall proceed in the same manner as in the case of an application by the Board under subsection (e) of this section, and shall have the same jurisdiction to grant to the Board such temporary relief or restraining order as it deems just and proper, and in like manner to make and enter a decree enforcing, modifying, and enforcing as so modified, or setting aside in whole or in part the order of the Board; the findings of the Board with respect to questions of fact if supported by *substantial* evidence *on the record considered as a whole* shall in like manner be conclusive.

(g) The commencement of proceedings under subsection (e) or (f) of this section shall not, unless specifically ordered by the court, operate as a stay of the Board's order.

(h) When granting appropriate temporary relief or a restraining order, or making and entering a decree enforcing, modifying, and enforcing as so modified, or setting aside in whole or in part an order of the Board, as provided in this section, the jurisdiction of courts sitting in equity shall not be limited by the Act entitled "An Act to amend the Judicial Code and to define and limit the jurisdiction of courts sitting in equity, and for other purposes," approved March 23, 1932 (U.S.C., Supp. VII, title 29, secs. 101–115).

[(i) Petitions filed under this Act shall be heard expeditiously, and if possible within ten days after they have been docketed.] *

*(j) The Board shall have power, upon issuance of a complaint as provided in subsection (b) charging that any person has engaged in or is engaging in an unfair labor practice, to petition any district court of the United States (including the District Court of the United States for the District of Columbia), within any district wherein the unfair labor practice in question is alleged to have occurred or wherein such*

* Section 10(i) was repealed by Pub.L. No.
98–260, § 402(31), 98 Stat. 3360 (1984).

*person resides or transacts business, for appropriate temporary relief or restraining order. Upon the filing of any such petition the court shall cause notice thereof to be served upon such person, and thereupon shall have jurisdiction to grant to the Board such temporary relief or restraining order as it deems just and proper.*

*(k) Whenever it is charged that any person has engaged in an unfair labor practice within the meaning of paragraph (4) (D) of section 8(b), the Board is empowered and directed to hear and determine the dispute out of which such unfair labor practice shall have arisen, unless, within ten days after notice that such charge has been filed, the parties to such dispute submit to the Board satisfactory evidence that they have adjusted, or agreed upon methods for the voluntary adjustment of, the dispute. Upon compliance by the parties to the dispute with the decision of the Board or upon such voluntary adjustment of the dispute, such charge shall be dismissed.*

*(l) Whenever it is charged that any person has engaged in an unfair labor practice within the meaning of paragraph (4)(A), (B), or (C) of section 8(b),* or section 8(e) or section 8(b)(7), *the preliminary investigation of such charge shall be made forthwith and given priority over all other cases except cases of like character in the office where it is filed or to which it is referred. If, after such investigation, the officer or regional attorney to whom the matter may be referred has reasonable cause to believe such charge is true and that a complaint should issue, he shall, on behalf of the Board, petition any district court of the United States (including the District Court of the United States for the District of Columbia) within any district where the unfair labor practice in question has occurred, is alleged to have occurred, or wherein such person resides or transacts business, for appropriate injunctive relief pending the final adjudication of the Board with respect to such matter. Upon the filing of any such petition the district court shall have jurisdiction to grant such injunctive relief or temporary restraining order as it deems just and proper, notwithstanding any other provision of law: Provided further, That no temporary restraining order shall be issued without notice unless a petition alleges that substantial and irreparable injury to the charging party will be unavoidable and such temporary restraining order shall be effective for no longer than five days and will become void at the expiration of such period:* Provided further, That such officer or regional attorney shall not apply for any restraining order under section 8(b) (7) if a charge against the employer under section 8(a) (2) has been filed and after the preliminary investigation, he has reasonable cause to believe that such charge is true and that a complaint should issue. *Upon filing of any such petition the courts shall cause notice thereof to be served upon any person involved in the charge and such person, including the charging party, shall be given an opportunity to appear by counsel and present any relevant testimony: Provided further, That for the purposes of this subsection district courts*

*shall be deemed to have jurisdiction of a labor organization (1) in the district in which such organization maintains its principal office, or (2) in any district in which its duly authorized officers or agents are engaged in promoting or protecting the interests of employee members. The service of legal process upon such officer or agent shall constitute service upon the labor organization and make such organization a party to the suit. In situations where such relief is appropriate the procedure specified herein shall apply to charges with respect to section 8(b) (4) (D).*

(m) Whenever it is charged that any person has engaged in an unfair labor practice within the meaning of subsection (a)(3) or (b) (2) of section 8, such charge shall be given priority over all other cases except cases of like character in the office where it is filed or to which it is referred and cases given priority under subsection (*l*).

## Investigatory Powers

**Sec. 11.** For the purpose of all hearings and investigations, which, in the opinion of the Board, are necessary and proper for the exercise of the powers vested in it by section 9 and section 10—

(1) The Board, or its duly authorized agents or agencies, shall at all reasonable times have access to, for the purpose of examination, and the right to copy any evidence of any person being investigated or proceeded against that relates to any matter under investigation or in question. The Board, or any member thereof, shall upon application of any party to such proceedings, forthwith issue to such party subpenas requiring the attendance and testimony of witnesses or the production of any evidence in such proceeding or investigation requested in such application. *Within five days after the service of a subpena on any person requiring the production of any evidence in his possession or under his control, such person may petition the Board to revoke, and the Board shall revoke, such subpena if in its opinion the evidence whose production is required does not relate to any matter under investigation, or any matter in question in such proceedings, or if in its opinion such subpena does not describe with sufficient particularity the evidence whose production is required.* Any member of the Board, or any agent or agency designated by the Board for such purposes, may administer oaths and affirmations, examine witnesses, and receive evidence. Such attendance of witnesses and the production of such evidence may be required from any place in the United States or any Territory or possession thereof, at any designated place of hearing.

(2) In case of contumacy, or refusal to obey a subpena issued to any person, any district court of the United States or the United States courts of any Territory or possession, or the District Court of the United States for the District of Columbia,

within the jurisdiction of which the inquiry is carried on or within the jurisdiction of which said person guilty of contumacy or refusal to obey is found or resides or transacts business, upon application by the Board shall have jurisdiction to issue to such person an order requiring such person to appear before the Board, its member, agent, or agency, there to produce evidence if so ordered, or there to give testimony touching the matter under investigation or in question; and any failure to obey such order of the court may be punished by said court as a contempt thereof.

(3) No person shall be excused from attending and testifying or from producing books, records, correspondence, documents, or other evidence in obedience to the subpena of the Board, on the ground that the testimony or evidence required of him may tend to incriminate him or subject him to a penalty or forfeiture; but no individual shall be prosecuted or subjected to any penalty or forfeiture for or on account of any transaction, matter, or thing concerning which he is compelled, after having claimed his privilege against self-incrimination, to testify or produce evidence, except that such individual so testifying shall not be exempt from prosecution and punishment for perjury committed in so testifying.*

(4) Complaints, orders, and other process and papers of the Board, its member, agent, or agency, may be served either personally or by registered or certified mail or by telegraph or by leaving a copy thereof at the principal office or place of business of the person required to be served. The verified return by the individual so serving the same setting forth the manner of such service shall be proof of the same, and the return post office receipt or telegraph receipt therefor when registered or certified and mailed or telegraphed as aforesaid shall be proof of service of the same. Witnesses summoned before the Board, its member, agent, or agency, shall be paid the same fees and mileage that are paid witnesses in the courts of the United States, and witnesses whose depositions are taken and the persons taking the same shall severally be entitled to the same fees as are paid for like services in the courts of the United States.

(5) All process of any court to which application may be made under this Act may be served in the judicial district wherein the defendant or other person required to be served resides or may be found.

(6) The several departments and agencies of the Government, when directed by the President, shall furnish the Board, upon its request, all records, papers, and information in their possession relating to any matter before the Board.

* Section 11(3) was repealed by Act of October 15, 1970, § 234, 84 Stat. 930. The Act substitutes for Section 11(3) similar immunity provisions. See 18 U.S.C. §§ 6001, 6002, 6004 (1982).

**Sec. 12.** Any person who shall willfully resist, prevent, impede, or interfere with any member of the Board or any of its agents or agencies in the performance of duties pursuant to this Act shall be punished by a fine of not more than $5,000 or by imprisonment for not more than one year, or both.

## LIMITATIONS

**Sec. 13.** Nothing in this Act, *except as specifically provided for herein,* shall be construed so as either to interfere with or impede or diminish in any way the right to strike, *or to affect the limitations or qualifications on that right.*

**Sec. 14.** *(a) Nothing herein shall prohibit any individual employed as a supervisor from becoming or remaining a member of a labor organization, but no employer subject to this Act shall be compelled to deem individuals defined herein as supervisors as employees for the purpose of any law, either national or local, relating to collective bargaining.*

*(b) Nothing in this Act shall be construed as authorizing the execution or application of agreements requiring membership in a labor organization as a condition of employment in any State or Territory in which such execution or application is prohibited by State or Territorial law.*

(c) (1) The Board, in its discretion, may, by rule of decision or by published rules adopted pursuant to the Administrative Procedure Act, decline to assert jurisdiction over any labor dispute involving any class or category of employers, where, in the opinion of the Board, the effect of such labor dispute on commerce is not sufficiently substantial to warrant the exercise of its jurisdiction: Provided, That the Board shall not decline to assert jurisdiction over any labor dispute over which it would assert jurisdiction under the standards prevailing upon August 1, 1959.

(2) Nothing in this Act shall be deemed to prevent or bar any agency or the courts of any State or Territory (including the Commonwealth of Puerto Rico, Guam, and the Virgin Islands), from assuming and asserting jurisdiction over labor disputes over which the Board declines, pursuant to paragraph (1) of this subsection, to assert jurisdiction.

**Sec. 15.** *Wherever the application of the provisions of section 272 of chapter 10 of the Act entitled "An Act to establish a uniform system of bankruptcy throughout the United States", approved July 1, 1898, and Acts amendatory thereof and supplementary thereto (U.S.C., title 11, sec. 672), conflicts with the application of the provisions of this Act, this Act shall prevail: Provided, That in any situation where the provisions of this Act cannot be validly enforced, the provisions of such other Acts shall remain in full force and effect.*

**Sec. 16.** If any provision of this Act, or the application of such provision to any person or circumstances, shall be held invalid, the remainder of this Act, or the application of such provision to persons or circumstances other than those as to which it is held invalid, shall not be affected thereby.

**Sec. 17.**    This Act may be cited as the "National Labor Relations Act".

**Sec. 18.***    No petition entertained, no investigation made, no election held, and no certification issued by the National Labor Relations Board, under any of the provisions of section 159 of this title, shall be invalid by reason of the failure of the Congress of Industrial Organizations to have complied with the requirements of section 9(f), (g), or (h) of this title prior to December 22, 1949, or by reason of the failure of the American Federation of Labor to have complied with the provisions of section 9(f), (g), or (h) of this title prior to November 7, 1947: *Provided,* That no liability shall be imposed under any provision of this chapter upon any person for failure to honor any election or certificate referred to above, prior to October 22, 1951: *Provided, however,* That this proviso shall not have the effect of setting aside or in any way affecting judgments or decrees heretofore entered under section 10(e) or (f) of this title and which have become final.

**Sec. 19.    Any employee [of a health care institution] ** who is a member of and adheres to established and traditional tenets or teachings of a bona fide religion, body, or sect which has historically held conscientious objections to joining or financially supporting labor organizations shall not be required to join or financially support any labor organization as a condition of employment; except that such employee may be required <u>in a contract between such employees' employer and a labor organization</u> in lieu of periodic dues and initiation fees, to pay sums equal to such dues and initiation fees to a nonreligious, <u>nonlabor organization</u> charitable fund exempt from taxation under section 501 (c)(3) <u>of title 26</u> of the Internal Revenue Code, chosen by such employee from a list of at least three such funds, designated in [a] such contract [between such institution and a labor organization] or if the contract fails to designate such funds, then to any such fund chosen by the employee. <u>If such employee who holds conscientious objections pursuant to this section requests the labor organization to use the grievance–arbitration procedure on the employee's behalf, the labor organization is authorized to charge the employee for the reasonable cost of using such procedure.</u>**

---

* This Section was made obsolete by the repeal, in 1959, of Section 9(f), (g), and (h).

** This section was amended by Pub.L.No. 96–593, 94 Stat. 3452 (1980). Deleted language is in brackets; new language added by the amendment is underscored.

# LABOR MANAGEMENT RELATIONS ACT

61 Stat. 136 (1947), as amended by 73 Stat. 519 (1959);
29 U.S.C. §§ 141–97 (1982).

## AN ACT

To amend the National Labor Relations Act, to provide additional facilities for the mediation of labor disputes affecting commerce, to equalize legal responsibilities of labor organizations and employers, and for other purposes.

*Be it enacted by the Senate and House of Representatives of the United States of America in Congress assembled,*

### SHORT TITLE AND DECLARATION OF POLICY

**Sec. 1.**  (a) This Act may be cited as the "Labor Management Relations Act, 1947."

(b) Industrial strife which interferes with the normal flow of commerce and with the full production of articles and commodities for commerce, can be avoided or substantially minimized if employers, employees, and labor organizations each recognize under law one another's legitimate rights in their relations with each other, and above all recognize under law that neither party has any right in its relations with any other to engage in acts or practices which jeopardize the public health, safety, or interest.

It is the purpose and policy of this Act, in order to promote the full flow of commerce, to prescribe the legitimate rights of both employees and employers in their relations affecting commerce, to provide orderly and peaceful procedures for preventing the interference by either with the legitimate rights of the other, to protect the rights of individual employees in their relations with labor organizations whose activities affect commerce, to define and proscribe practices on the part of labor and management which affect commerce and are inimical to the general welfare, and to protect the rights of the public in connection with labor disputes affecting commerce.

## TITLE I

### AMENDMENT OF NATIONAL LABOR RELATIONS ACT

**Sec. 101.**  The National Labor Relations Act is hereby amended to read as follows: [The text of the National Labor Relations Act as amended is set forth supra.]

## TITLE II

CONCILIATION OF LABOR DISPUTES IN INDUSTRIES AFFECTING
COMMERCE; NATIONAL EMERGENCIES

**Sec. 201.** That it is the policy of the United States that—

(a) sound and stable industrial peace and the advancement of the general welfare, health, and safety of the Nation and of the best interests of employers and employees can most satisfactorily be secured by the settlement of issues between employers and employees through the processes of conference and collective bargaining between employers and the representatives of their employees;

(b) the settlement of issues between employers and employees through collective bargaining may be advanced by making available full and adequate governmental facilities for conciliation, mediation, and voluntary arbitration to aid and encourage employers and the representatives of their employees to reach and maintain agreements concerning rates of pay, hours, and working conditions, and to make all reasonable efforts to settle their differences by mutual agreement reached through conferences and collective bargaining or by such methods as may be provided for in any applicable agreement for the settlement of disputes; and

(c) certain controversies which arise between parties to collective-bargaining agreements may be avoided or minimized by making available full and adequate governmental facilities for furnishing assistance to employers and the representatives of their employees in formulating for inclusion within such agreements provision for adequate notice of any proposed changes in the terms of such agreements, for the final adjustment of grievances or questions regarding the application or interpretation of such agreements, and other provisions designed to prevent the subsequent arising of such controversies.

**Sec. 202.** (a) There is hereby created an independent agency to be known as the Federal Mediation and Conciliation Service (herein referred to as the "Service," except that for sixty days after the date of the enactment of this Act such term shall refer to the Conciliation Service of the Department of Labor). The Service shall be under the direction of a Federal Mediation and Conciliation Director (hereinafter referred to as the "Director"), who shall be appointed by the President by and with the advice and consent of the Senate. The Director shall receive compensation at the rate of $12,000 * per annum.

---

* As of January 1, 1984, the salary of the
Director became $70,800. See 5 U.S.
C.A. § 5314 (and note following) (West
Supp. 1985).

The Director shall not engage in any other business, vocation, or employment.

(b) The Director is authorized, subject to the civil-service laws, to appoint such clerical and other personnel as may be necessary for the execution of the functions of the Service, and shall fix their compensation in accordance with chapter 51 and subchapter III of chapter 53 of title 5, and may, without regard to the provisions of the civil-service laws, appoint such conciliators and mediators as may be necessary to carry out the functions of the Service. The Director is authorized to make such expenditures for supplies, facilities, and services as he deems necessary. Such expenditures shall be allowed and paid upon presentation of itemized vouchers therefor approved by the Director or by any employee designated by him for that purpose.

(c) The principal office of the Service shall be in the District of Columbia, but the Director may establish regional offices convenient to localities in which labor controversies are likely to arise. The Director may by order, subject to revocation at any time, delegate any authority and discretion conferred upon him by this Act to any regional director, or other officer or employee of the Service. The Director may establish suitable procedures for cooperation with State and local mediation agencies. The Director shall make an annual report in writing to Congress at the end of the fiscal year.

(d) All mediation and conciliation functions of the Secretary of Labor or the United States Conciliation Service under section 8 of the Act entitled "An Act to create a Department of Labor," approved March 4, 1913 (U.S.C., title 29, sec. 51), and all functions of the United States Conciliation Service under any other law are hereby transferred to the Federal Mediation and Conciliation Service, together with the personnel and records of the United States Conciliation Service. Such transfer shall take effect upon the sixtieth day after the date of enactment of this Act. Such transfer shall not affect any proceedings pending before the United States Conciliation Service or any certification, order, rule, or regulation theretofore made by it or by the Secretary of Labor. The Director and the Service shall not be subject in any way to the jurisdiction or authority of the Secretary of Labor or any official or division of the Department of Labor.

### FUNCTIONS OF THE SERVICE

Sec. 203. (a) It shall be the duty of the Service, in order to prevent or minimize interruptions of the free flow of commerce growing out of labor disputes, to assist parties to labor disputes in industries affecting commerce to settle such disputes through conciliation and mediation.

(b) The Service may proffer its services in any labor dispute in any industry affecting commerce, either upon its own motion or upon the request of one or more of the parties to the dispute, whenever in its judgment such dispute threatens to cause a substantial interruption of commerce. The Director and the Service are directed to avoid attempting to mediate disputes which would have only a minor effect on interstate commerce if State or other conciliation services are available to the parties. Whenever the Service does proffer its services in any dispute, it shall be the duty of the Service promptly to put itself in communication with the parties and to use its best efforts, by mediation and conciliation, to bring them to agreement.

(c) If the Director is not able to bring the parties to agreement by conciliation within a reasonable time, he shall seek to induce the parties voluntarily to seek other means of settling the dispute without resort to strike, lock-out, or other coercion, including submission to the employees in the bargaining unit of the employer's last offer of settlement for approval or rejection in a secret ballot. The failure or refusal of either party to agree to any procedure suggested by the Director shall not be deemed a violation of any duty or obligation imposed by this Act.

(d) Final adjustment by a method agreed upon by the parties is hereby declared to be the desirable method for settlement of grievance disputes arising over the application or interpretation of an existing collective-bargaining agreement. The Service is directed to make its conciliation and mediation services available in the settlement of such grievance disputes only as a last resort and in exceptional cases.

(e) The Service is authorized and directed to encourage and support the establishment and operation of joint labor management activities conducted by plant, area, and industrywide committees designed to improve labor management relationships, job security and organizational effectiveness, in accordance with the provisions of section 205A.*

**Sec. 204.** (a) In order to prevent or minimize interruptions of the free flow of commerce growing out of labor disputes, employers and employees and their representatives, in any industry affecting commerce, shall—

(1) exert every reasonable effort to make and maintain agreements concerning rates of pay, hours, and working conditions, including provision for adequate notice of any proposed change in the terms of such agreements;

(2) whenever a dispute arises over the terms or application of a collective-bargaining agreement and a conference is requested by a party or prospective party thereto, arrange promptly for such a conference to be held and endeavor in such conference to settle such dispute expeditiously; and

(3) in case such dispute is not settled by conference, participate fully and promptly in such meetings as may be undertaken

---

\* Subsection (e) was enacted by Pub.L.No.
95–524, § 6 (c)(1), 92 Stat. 2020 (1978).

by the Service under this Act for the purpose of aiding in a settlement of the dispute.

**Sec. 205.** (a) There is hereby created a National Labor-Management Panel which shall be composed of twelve members appointed by the President, six of whom shall be selected from among persons outstanding in the field of management and six of whom shall be selected from among persons outstanding in the field of labor. Each member shall hold office for a term of three years, except that any member appointed to fill a vacancy occurring prior to the expiration of the term for which his predecessor was appointed shall be appointed for the remainder of such term, and the terms of office of the members first taking office shall expire, as designated by the President at the time of appointment, four at the end of the first year, four at the end of the second year, and four at the end of the third year after the date of appointment. Members of the panel, when serving on business of the panel, shall be paid compensation at the rate of $25 per day, and shall also be entitled to receive an allowance for actual and necessary travel and subsistence expenses while so serving away from their places of residence.

(b) It shall be the duty of the panel, at the request of the Director, to advise in the avoidance of industrial controversies and the manner in which mediation and voluntary adjustment shall be administered, particularly with reference to controversies affecting the general welfare of the country.

Sec. 205A. (a) (1) The Service is authorized and directed to provide assistance in the establishment and operation of plant, area and industrywide labor management committees which—

(A) have been organized jointly by employers and labor organizations representing employees in that plant, area, or industry; and

(B) are established for the purpose of improving labor management relationships, job security, organizational effectiveness, enhancing economic development or involving workers in decisions affecting their jobs including improving communication with respect to subjects of mutual interest and concern.

(2) The Service is authorized and directed to enter into contracts and to make grants, where necessary or appropriate, to fulfill its responsibilities under this section.

(b) (1) No grant may be made, no contract may be entered into and no other assistance may be provided under the provisions of this section to a plant labor management committee unless the employees in that plant are represented by a labor organization and there is in effect at that plant a collective bargaining agreement.

(2) No grant may be made, no contract may be entered into and no other assistance may be provided under the provisions of

this section to an area or industrywide labor management committee unless its participants include any labor organizations certified or recognized as the representative of the employees of an employer participating in such committee. Nothing in this clause shall prohibit participation in an area or industrywide committee by an employer whose employees are not represented by a labor organization.

(3) No grant may be made under the provisions of this section to any labor management committee which the Service finds to have as one of its purposes the discouragement of the exercise of rights contained in section 7 of the National Labor Relations Act (29 U.S.C. 157), or the interference with collective bargaining in any plant, or industry.

(c) The Service shall carry out the provisions of this section through an office established for that purpose.

(d) There are authorized to be appropriated to carry out the provisions of this section $10,000,000 for the fiscal year 1979, and such sums as may be necessary thereafter.*

## National Emergencies

**Sec. 206.** Whenever in the opinion of the President of the United States, a threatened or actual strike or lock-out affecting an entire industry or a substantial part thereof engaged in trade, commerce, transportation, transmission, or communication among the several States or with foreign nations, or engaged in the production of goods for commerce, will, if permitted to occur or to continue, imperil the national health or safety, he may appoint a board of inquiry to inquire into the issues involved in the dispute and to make a written report to him within such time as he shall prescribe. Such report shall include a statement of the facts with respect to the dispute, including each party's statement of its position but shall not contain any recommendations. The President shall file a copy of such report with the Service and shall make its contents available to the public.

**Sec. 207.** (a) A board of inquiry shall be composed of a chairman and such other members as the President shall determine, and shall have power to sit and act in any place within the United States and to conduct such hearings either in public or in private, as it may deem necessary or proper, to ascertain the facts with respect to the causes and circumstances of the dispute.

(b) Members of a board of inquiry shall receive compensation at the rate of $50 for each day actually spent by them in the work of the board, together with necessary travel and subsistence expenses.

(c) For the purpose of any hearing or inquiry conducted by any board appointed under this title, the provisions of sections 9 and 10 (relating to the attendance of witnesses and the production of books,

* Section 205A was enacted by Pub.L.No.
  95–524, § 6 (c)(2), 92 Stat. 2020 (1978).

papers, and documents) of the Federal Trade Commission Act of September 16, 1914, as amended (U.S.C. 19, title 15, secs. 49 and 50, as amended), are hereby made applicable to the powers and duties of such board.

Sec. 208. (a) Upon receiving a report from a board of inquiry the President may direct the Attorney General to petition any district court of the United States having jurisdiction of the parties to enjoin such strike or lock-out or the continuing thereof, and if the court finds that such threatened or actual strike or lock-out—

(i) affects an entire industry or a substantial part thereof engaged in trade, commerce, transportation, transmission, or communication among the several States or with foreign nations, or engaged in the production of goods for commerce; and

(ii) if permitted to occur or to continue, will imperil the national health or safety, it shall have jurisdiction to enjoin any such strike or lock-out, or the continuing thereof, and to make such other orders as may be appropriate.

(b) In any case, the provisions of the Act of March 23, 1932, entitled "An Act to amend the Judicial Code and to define and limit the jurisdiction of courts sitting in equity, and for other purposes," shall not be applicable.

(c) The order or orders of the court shall be subject to review by the appropriate United States court of appeals and by the Supreme Court upon writ of certiorari or certification as provided in sections 239 and 240 of the Judicial Code, as amended (U.S.C., title 29, secs. 346 and 347).

Sec. 209. (a) Whenever a district court has issued an order under section 208 enjoining acts or practices which imperil or threaten to imperil the national health or safety, it shall be the duty of the parties to the labor dispute giving rise to such order to make every effort to adjust and settle their differences, with the assistance of the Service created by this Act. Neither party shall be under any duty to accept, in whole or in part, any proposal of settlement made by the Service.

(b) Upon the issuance of such order, the President shall reconvene the board of inquiry which has previously reported with respect to the dispute. At the end of a sixty-day period (unless the dispute has been settled by that time), the board of inquiry shall report to the President the current position of the parties and the efforts which have been made for settlement, and shall include a statement by each party of its position and a statement of the employer's last offer of settlement. The President shall make such report available to the public. The National Labor Relations Board, within the succeeding fifteen days, shall take a secret ballot of the employees of each employer involved in the dispute on the question of whether they wish to accept the final offer of settlement made by their employer as stated by him and shall certify the results thereof to the Attorney General within five days thereafter.

Sec. 210. Upon the certification of the results of such ballot or upon a settlement being reached, whichever happens sooner, the Attorney General shall move the court to discharge the injunction, which motion shall then be granted and the injunction discharged. When such motion is granted, the President shall submit to the Congress a full and comprehensive report of the proceedings, including the findings of the board of inquiry and the ballot taken by the National Labor Relations Board, together with such recommendations as he may see fit to make for consideration and appropriate action.

## COMPILATION OF COLLECTIVE BARGAINING AGREEMENTS, ETC.

Sec. 211. (a) For the guidance and information of interested representatives of employers, employees, and the general public, the Bureau of Labor Statistics of the Department of Labor shall maintain a file of copies of all available collective-bargaining agreements and other available agreements and actions thereunder settling or adjusting labor disputes. Such file shall be open to inspection under appropriate conditions prescribed by the Secretary of Labor, except that no specific information submitted in confidence shall be disclosed.

(b) The Bureau of Labor Statistics in the Department of Labor is authorized to furnish upon request of the Service, or employers, employees, or their representatives, all available data and factual information which may aid in the settlement of any labor dispute, except that no specific information submitted in confidence shall be disclosed.

## EXEMPTION OF RAILWAY LABOR ACT

Sec. 212. The provisions of this title shall not be applicable with respect to any matter which is subject to the provisions of the Railway Labor Act, as amended from time to time.

## CONCILIATION OF LABOR DISPUTES IN THE HEALTH CARE INDUSTRY

Sec. 213. (a) If, in the opinion of the Director of the Federal Mediation and Conciliation Service a threatened or actual strike or lockout affecting a health care institution will, if permitted to occur or to continue, substantially interrupt the delivery of health care in the locality concerned, the Director may further assist in the resolution of the impasse by establishing within 30 days after the notice to the Federal Mediation and Conciliation Service under clause (A) of the last sentence of section 8(d) (which is required by clause (3) of such section 8(d) ), or within 10 days after the notice under clause (B), an impartial Board of Inquiry to investigate the issues involved in the dispute and to make a written report thereon to the parties within fifteen (15) days after the establishment of such a Board. The written report shall contain the findings of fact together with the Board's recommendations for settling the dispute, with the objective of achieving a prompt, peaceful and just settlement of the dispute. Each such Board shall be composed of such number of individuals as the Director may deem desirable. No member appointed under this section shall have any interest or involvement in the health care institutions or the employee organizations involved in the dispute.

(b)(1) Members of any board established under this section who are otherwise employed by the Federal Government shall serve without compensation but shall be reimbursed for travel, subsistence, and other necessary expenses incurred by them in carrying out its duties under this section.

(2) Members of any board established under this section who are not subject to paragraph (1) shall receive compensation at a rate prescribed by the Director but not to exceed the daily rate prescribed for GS–18 of the General Schedule under section 5332 of title 5, United States Code, including travel for each day they are engaged in the performance of their duties under this section and shall be entitled to reimbursement for travel, subsistence, and other necessary expenses incurred by them in carrying out their duties under this section.

(c) After the establishment of a board under subsection (a) of this section and for 15 days after any such board has issued its report, no change in the status quo in effect prior to the expiration of the contract in the case of negotiations for a contract renewal, or in effect prior to the time of the impasse in the case of an initial bargaining negotiation, except by agreement, shall be made by the parties to the controversy.

(d) There are authorized to be appropriated such sums as may be necessary to carry out the provisions of this section.*

## TITLE III

### SUITS BY AND AGAINST LABOR ORGANIZATIONS

**Sec. 301.** (a) Suits for violation of contracts between an employer and a labor organization representing employees in an industry affecting commerce as defined in this Act, or between any such labor organizations, may be brought in any district court of the United States having jurisdiction of the parties, without respect to the amount in controversy or without regard to the citizenship of the parties.

---

* Section 213 was enacted by Pub.L.No. 93–360, § 2, 88 Stat. 396 (1974).

**(b)** Any labor organization which represents employees in an industry affecting commerce as defined in this Act and any employer whose activities affect commerce as defined in this Act shall be bound by the acts of its agents. Any such labor organization may sue or be sued as an entity and in behalf of the employees whom it represents in the courts of the United States. Any money judgment against a labor organization in a district court of the United States shall be enforceable only against the organization as an entity and against its assets, and shall not be enforceable against any individual member or his assets.

**(c)** For the purposes of actions and proceedings by or against labor organizations in the district courts of the United States, district courts shall be deemed to have jurisdiction of a labor organization (1) in the district in which such organization maintains its principal office, or (2) in any district in which its duly authorized officers or agents are engaged in representing or acting for employee members.

**(d)** The service of summons, subpena, or other legal process of any court of the United States upon an officer or agent of a labor organization, in his capacity as such, shall constitute service upon the labor organization.

**(e)** For the purposes of this section, in determining whether any person is acting as an "agent" of another person so as to make such other person responsible for his acts, the question of whether the specific acts performed were actually authorized or subsequently ratified shall not be controlling.

### Restrictions on Payments to Employee Representatives

**Sec. 302.**   **(a)** It shall be unlawful for any employer or association of employers or any person who acts as a labor relations expert, adviser, or consultant to an employer or who acts in the interest of an employer to pay, lend, or deliver, or agree to pay, lend, or deliver, any money or other thing of value—

(1) to any representative of any of his employees who are employed in an industry affecting commerce; or

(2) to any labor organization, or any officer or employee thereof, which represents, seeks to represent, or would admit to membership, any of the employees of such employer who are employed in an industry affecting commerce; or

(3) to any employee or group or committee of employees of such employer employed in an industry affecting commerce in excess of their normal compensation for the purpose of causing such employee or group or committee directly or indirectly to influence any other employees in the exercise of the right to organize and bargain collectively through representatives of their own choosing; or

(4) to any officer or employee of a labor organization engaged in an industry affecting commerce with intent to influence him in respect to any of his actions, decisions, or duties as a representative of employees or as such officer or employee of such labor organization.

(b) (1) It shall be unlawful for any person to request, demand, receive, or accept, or agree to receive or accept, any payment, loan, or delivery of any money or other thing of value prohibited by subsection (a).

(2) It shall be unlawful for any labor organization, or for any person acting as an officer, agent, representative, or employee of such labor organization, to demand or accept from the operator of any motor vehicle (as defined in part II of the Interstate Commerce Act) employed in the transportation of property in commerce, or the employer of any such operator, any money or other thing of value payable to such organization or to an officer, agent, representative or employee thereof as a fee or charge for the unloading, or in connection with the unloading, of the cargo of such vehicle: Provided, That nothing in this paragraph shall be construed to make unlawful any payment by an employer to any of his employees as compensation for their services as employees.

(c) The provisions of this section shall not be applicable (1) in respect to any money or other thing of value payable by an employer to any of his employees whose established duties include acting openly for such employer in matters of labor relations or personnel administration or to any representative of his employees, or to any officer or employee of a labor organization, who is also an employee or former employee of such employer, as compensation for, or by reason of, his service as an employee of such employer; (2) with respect to the payment or delivery of any money or other thing of value in satisfaction of a judgment of any court or a decision or award of an arbitrator or impartial chairman or in compromise, adjustment, settlement, or release of any claim, complaint, grievance, or dispute in the absence of fraud or duress; (3) with respect to the sale or purchase of an article or commodity at the prevailing market price in the regular course of business; (4) with respect to money deducted from the wages of employees in payment of membership dues in a labor organization: Provided, That the employer has received from each employee, on whose account such deductions are made, a written assignment which shall not be irrevocable for a period of more than one year, or beyond the termination date of the applicable collective agreement, whichever occurs sooner; (5) with respect to money or other thing of value paid to a trust fund established by such representative, for the sole and exclusive benefit of the employees of such employer, and their families and dependents (or of such employees, families, and dependents jointly with the employees of other employers making similar payments, and their families and dependents): Provided, That (A) such payments are held in trust for the purpose of paying, either from principal or income or both, for the benefit of employees, their families and dependents, for medical or hospital care, pensions on retirement or death of employees, compensation for injuries or illness resulting from occupational activity or insurance to provide any of the foregoing, or unemployment benefits or life insurance, disability and sickness insurance, or accident insurance;  (B) the detailed basis on which such payments are to be made is specified in a written agreement with the employer, and employees and employers are equally represented in the administration of such fund, together with such neutral persons as the representatives of the employers and the representatives of employees may agree upon and in the event the employer and employee groups deadlock on the administration of such fund and there are no neutral persons empowered to break such deadlock, such agreement provides that the two groups shall agree on an impartial umpire to decide such dispute, or in event of their failure to agree within a reasonable length of time, an impartial umpire to decide such dispute shall, on petition of either group, be appointed by the district court of the United States for the district where the trust fund has its principal office, and shall also contain provisions for an annual audit of the trust fund, a statement of the results of which shall be available for inspection by interested persons at the principal office of the trust fund and at such other places as may be designated in such written agreement; and (C) such payments as are intended to be used for the purpose of providing pensions or annuities for employees are made to a separate trust which provides that the funds held therein cannot be used for any purpose other than paying such pensions or annuities;  (6) with respect to money or other thing of value paid by any employer to a trust fund established by such representative for the purpose of pooled vacation, holiday, severance or similar benefits, or defraying costs of apprenticeship or other training programs: Provided, That the requirements of clause (B) of the proviso to clause (5) of this subsection, shall apply to such trust funds; (7) with respect to money or other thing of value paid by any employer to a pooled or individual trust fund established by such representative for the purpose of (A) scholarships for the benefit of employees, their families, and dependents for study at educational institutions, or (B) child care centers for pre-school and school age dependents of employees: *Provided,* That no labor organization or employer shall be required to bargain on the establishment of any such trust fund, and refusal to do so shall not constitute an unfair labor practice: *Provided further,* That the requirements of clause (B) of the proviso to clause (5) of this subsection shall apply to such trust funds; (8) with respect to money or any other thing of value paid by any employer to a trust fund established by such representative for the purpose of defraying the costs of legal services for employees, their families, and dependents for counsel or plan of their choice: *Provided,* That the requirements of clause (B) of the proviso to clause (5) of this subsection shall apply to such trust funds: *Provided* *further,* That no such legal services shall be furnished: (A) to initiate any proceeding directed (i) against any such employer or its officers or agents except in workman's compensation cases, or (ii) against such labor organization, or its parent or subordinate bodies, or their officers or agents, or (iii) against any other employer or labor organization, or their officers or agents, in any matter arising under the National Labor Relations Act, as amended, or this Act; and (B) in any proceeding where a labor organization would be prohibited from defraying the costs of legal services by the provisions of the Labor-Management Reporting and Disclosure Act of 1959; or (9) with respect to money or other things of value paid by an employer to a plant, area or industrywide labor management committee established for one or more of the purposes set forth in section 5 (b) of the Labor Management Cooperation Act of 1978.*

(d)(1) Any person who participates in a transaction involving a payment, loan, or delivery of money or other thing of value to a labor organization in payment of membership dues or to a joint labor-management trust fund as defined by clause (B) of the proviso to clause (5) of subsection (c) of this section or to a plant, area, or industry-wide labor-management committee that is received and used by such labor organization, trust fund, or committee, which transaction does not satisfy all the applicable requirements of subsections (c)(4) through (c)(9) of this section, and willfully and with intent to benefit himself or to benefit other persons he knows are not permitted to receive a payment, loan, money, or other thing of value under subsections (c)(4) through (c)(9) violates this subsection, shall, upon conviction thereof, be guilty of a felony and be subject to a fine of not more than $15,000, or imprisoned for not more than five years, or both; but if the value of the amount of money or thing of value involved in any violation of the provisions of this section does not exceed $1,000, such person shall be guilty of a misdemeanor and be subject to a fine of not more than $10,000, or imprisoned for not more than one year, or both.

(2) Except for violations involving transactions covered by subsection (d)(1) of this section, any person who willfully violates this section shall, upon conviction thereof, be guilty of a felony and be subject to a fine of not more than $15,000, or imprisoned for not more than five years, or both; but if the value of the amount of money or thing of value involved in any violation of the provisions of this section does not exceed $1,000, such person shall be guilty of a misdemeanor and be subject to a fine of not more than $10,000, or imprisoned for not more than one year, or both.**

* Clause (7) was enacted by Pub.L.No. 91–86, 83 Stat. 133 (1969). Clause (8) was enacted by Pub.L.No. 93–95, 87 Stat. 314 (1973). Clause (9) was enacted by Pub.L.No. 95–524, § 6 (d), 92 Stat. 2021 (1978).

** Subsection (d) was substantially amended by Pub.L.No. 98–473, § 801, 98 Stat. 2131 (1984).

(e) The district courts of the United States and the United States courts of the Territories and possessions shall have jurisdiction, for cause shown, and subject to the provisions of section 17 (relating to notice to opposite party) of the Act entitled "An Act to supplement existing laws against unlawful restraints and monopolies, and for other purposes," approved October 15, 1914, as amended (U.S.C., title 28, section 381), to restrain violations of this section, without regard to the provisions of sections 6 and 20 of such Act of October 15, 1914, as amended (U.S.C., title 15, section 17, and title 29, section 52), and the provisions of the Act entitled "An Act to amend the Judicial Code and to define and limit the jurisdiction of courts sitting in equity, and for other purposes," approved March 23, 1932 (U.S.C., title 29, sections 101–115).

(f) This section shall not apply to any contract in force on the date of enactment of this Act, until the expiration of such contract, or until July 1, 1948, whichever first occurs.

(g) Compliance with the restrictions contained in subsection (c) (5) (B) upon contributions to trust funds, otherwise lawful, shall not be applicable to contributions to such trust funds established by collective agreement prior to January 1, 1946, nor shall subsection (c) (5) (A) be construed as prohibiting contributions to such trust funds if prior to January 1, 1947, such funds contained provisions for pooled vacation benefits.

### BOYCOTTS AND OTHER UNLAWFUL COMBINATIONS

**Sec. 303.**    (a) It shall be unlawful, for the purpose of this section only, in an industry or activity affecting commerce, for any labor organization to engage in any activity or conduct defined as an unfair labor practice in section 8(b) (4) of the National Labor Relations Act, as amended.

(b) Whoever shall be injured in his business or property by reason of any violation of subsection (a) may sue therefor in any district court of the United States subject to the limitations and provisions of section 301 hereof without respect to the amount in controversy, or in any other court having jurisdiction of the parties, and shall recover the damages by him sustained and the cost of the suit.

### RESTRICTION ON POLITICAL CONTRIBUTIONS

**Sec. 304.**    Section 313 of the Federal Corrupt Practices Act, 1925 (U.S.C., 1940 edition, title 2, sec. 251; Supp. V, title 50, App., sec. 1509), as amended, is amended to read as follows:

Sec. 313.    It is unlawful for any national bank, or any corporation organized by authority of any law of Congress, to make a contribution or expenditure in connection with any election to any political office, or in connection with any primary election or political convention or caucus held to select candidates for any political office, or for any corporation whatever, or any labor organization to make a contribution or expenditure in connection with any election at which Presidential and Vice Presidential electors or a Senator or Representative in, or a Delegate or Resident Commissioner to Congress are to be voted for, or in connection with any primary election or political convention or caucus held to select candidates for any of the foregoing offices, or for any candidate, political committee, or other person to accept or receive any contribution prohibited by this section. Every corporation or labor organization which makes any contribution or expenditure in violation of this section shall be fined not more than $5,000; and every officer or director of any corporation, or officer of any labor organization, who consents to any contribution or expenditure by the corporation or labor organization, as the case may be, *and any person who accepts or receives any contribution*, in violation of this section shall be fined not more than $1,000 or imprisoned for not more than one year, or both; *and if the violation was willful, shall be fined not more than $10,000 or imprisoned not more than two years, or both.* For the purposes of this section "labor organization" means any organization of any kind, or any agency or employee representation committee or plan, in which employees participate and which exist for the purpose, in whole or in part, of dealing with employers concerning grievances, labor disputes, wages, rates of pay, hours of employment, or conditions of work. [The italicized provisions were added by Act of October 31, 1951, ch. 655, § 20(c), 65 Stat. 718.]*

---

* Section 313 of the Federal Corrupt Practices Act was later codified in 18 U.S.C. § 610 and then amended by Section 205 of the Federal Election Campaign Act of 1971, Pub.L. No. 92–225, 86 Stat. 3, Feb. 7, 1972. In 1976 Congress repealed Section 610 and incorporated limitations on corporate and union federal election campaign spending as a part of The Federal Election Campaign Act of 1976, Pub.L. No. 94–283, 90 Stat. 490, May 11, 1976. Section 321 of that act codifies as 2 U.S.C. § 441b the following limitations on union and corporate spending:

"Sec. 321. (a) It is unlawful for any national bank, or any corporation organized by authority of any law of Congress, to make a contribution or expenditure in connection with any election to any political office, or in connection with any primary election or political convention or caucus held to select candidates for any political office, or for any corporation whatever, or any labor organization, to make a contribution or expenditure in connection with any election at which presidential and vice presidential electors or a Senator or Representative in, or a Delegate or Resident Commissioner to, Congress are to be voted for, or in connection with any primary election or political convention or caucus held to select candidates for any of the foregoing offices, or for any candidate, political committee, or other person knowingly to accept or receive any contribution prohibited by this section, or any officer or any director of any corporation or any national bank or any officer of any labor organization to consent to any contribution or expenditure by the corporation, national bank, or labor organization, as the case may be, prohibited by this section.

"(b)(1) For the purposes of this section the term 'labor organization' means any organization of any kind, or any agency or employee representation committee or plan, in which employees participate and which exists for the purpose, in whole or in part, of dealing with employers concerning grievances, labor disputes, wages, rates of pay, hours of employment, or conditions of work.

"(2) For purposes of this section and section 12(h) of the Public Utility Holding Company Act (15 U.S.C. 791(h)), the term 'contribution or expenditure' shall include any direct or indirect payment, distribution, loan, advance, deposit, or gift of money, or any services, or anything of value (except a loan of money by a national or State bank made in accordance with the applicable banking laws and regulations and in the ordinary course of business) to any candidate, campaign committee, or political party or organization, in connection with any election to any of the offices referred to in this section, but shall not include (A) communications by a corporation to its stockholders and executive or administrative personnel and their families or by a labor organization to its members and their families on any subject; (B) nonpartisan registration and get-out-the-vote campaigns by a corporation aimed at its stockholders and executive or administrative personnel and their families, or by a labor organization aimed at its members and their families; and (C) the establishment, administration, and solicitation of contributions to a separate segregated fund to be utilized for political purposes by a corporation, labor organization, membership organization, cooperative, or corporation without capital stock.

"(3) It shall be unlawful—

"(A) for such a fund to make a contribution or expenditure by utilizing money or anything of value secured by physical force, job discrimination, financial reprisals, or the threat of force, job discrimination, or financial reprisal; or by dues, fees, or other moneys required as a condition of membership in a labor organiza-

tion or as a condition of employment, or by moneys obtained in any commercial transaction;

"(B) for any person soliciting an employee for a contribution to such a fund to fail to inform such employee of the political purposes of such fund at the time of such solicitation; and

"(C) for any person soliciting an employee for a contribution to such a fund to fail to inform such employee, at the time of such solicitation, of his right to refuse to so contribute without any reprisal.

"(4)(A) Except as provided in subparagraphs (B), (C), and (D), it shall be unlawful—

"(i) for a corporation, or a separate segregated fund established by a corporation, to solicit contributions to such a fund from any person other than its stockholders and their families and its executive or administrative personnel and their families, and

"(ii) for a labor organization, or a separate segregated fund established by a labor organization, to solicit contributions to such a fund from any person other than its members and their families.

"(B) It shall not be unlawful under this section for a corporation, a labor organization, or a separate segregated fund established by such corporation or such labor organization, to make 2 written solicitations for contributions during the calendar year from any stockholder, executive or administrative personnel, or employee of a corporation or the families of such persons. A solicitation under this subparagraph may be made only by mail addressed to stockholders, executive or administrative personnel, or employees at their residence and shall be so designed that the corporation, labor organization, or separate segregated fund conducting such solicitation cannot determine who makes a contribution of $50 or less as a result of such solicitation and who does not make such a contribution.

"(C) This paragraph shall not prevent a membership organization, cooperative, or corporation without

STRIKES BY GOVERNMENT EMPLOYEES

**Sec. 305.** It shall be unlawful for any individual employed by the United States or any agency thereof including wholly owned Government corporations to participate in any strike. Any individual employed by the United States or by any such agency who strikes shall be discharged immediately from his employment, and shall forfeit his civil-service status, if any, and shall not be eligible for reemployment for three years by the United States or any such agency.**

**TITLE IV**

CREATION OF JOINT COMMITTEE TO STUDY AND REPORT ON BASIC PROBLEMS AFFECTING FRIENDLY LABOR RELATIONS AND PRODUCTIVITY

\* \* \*

capital stock, or a separate segregated fund established by a membership organization, cooperative, or corporation without capital stock, from soliciting contributions to such a fund from members of such organization, cooperative, or corporation without capital stock.

"(D) This paragraph shall not prevent a trade association or a separate segregated fund established by a trade association from soliciting contributions from the stockholders and executive or administrative personnel of the member corporations of such trade association and the families of such stockholders or personnel to the extent that such solicitation of such stockholders and personnel, and their families, has been separately and specifically approved by the member corporation involved, and such member corporation does not approve any such solicitation by more than one such trade association in any calendar year.

"(5) Notwithstanding any other law, any method of soliciting voluntary contributions or of facilitating the making of voluntary contributions to a separate segregated fund established by a corporation, permitted by law to corporations with regard to stockholders and executive or administrative personnel, shall also be permitted to labor or-

ganizations with regard to their members.

"(6) Any corporation, including its subsidiaries, branches, divisions, and affiliates, that utilizes a method of soliciting voluntary contributions or facilitating the making of voluntary contributions, shall make available such method, on written request and at a cost sufficient only to reimburse the corporation for the expenses incurred thereby, to a labor organization representing any members working for such corporation, its subsidiaries, branches, divisions, and affiliates.

"(7) For purposes of this section, the term 'executive or administrative personnel' means individuals employed by a corporation who are paid on a salary, rather than hourly, basis and who have policymaking, managerial, professional, or supervisory responsibilities."

** Section 305 was repealed by Pub.L. No. 330, 69 Stat. 624 (1955), which substituted therefor the similar provisions of 5 U.S.C. §§ 118p–118r prohibiting strikes by public employees. The latter provisions were in turn replaced by 80 Stat. 424, 524, and 609 (1966), 5 U.S.C. §§ 3333, 7311, 18 U.S.C. § 1918 (1970) (discussed in United Federation of Postal Clerks v. Blount, reported in the casebook in Chapter 9, Section D).

## TITLE V

### DEFINITIONS

**Sec. 501.** When used in this Act—

(1) The term "industry affecting commerce" means any industry or activity in commerce or in which a labor dispute would burden or obstruct commerce or tend to burden or obstruct commerce or the free flow of commerce.

(2) The term "strike" includes any strike or other concerted stoppage of work by employees (including a stoppage by reason of the expiration of a collective-bargaining agreement) and any concerted slow-down or other concerted interruption of operations by employees.

(3) The terms "commerce", "labor disputes", "employer", "employee", "labor organization", "representative", "person", and "supervisor" shall have the same meaning as when used in the National Labor Relations Act as amended by this Act.

### SAVING PROVISION

**Sec. 502.** Nothing in this Act shall be construed to require an individual employee to render labor or service without his consent, nor shall anything in this Act be construed to make the quitting of his labor by an individual employee an illegal act; nor shall any court issue any process to compel the performance by an individual employee of such labor or service, without his consent; nor shall the quitting of labor by an employee or employees in good faith because of abnormally dangerous conditions for work at the place of employment of such employee or employees be deemed a strike under this Act.

### SEPARABILITY

**Sec. 503.** If any provision of this Act, or the application of such provision to any person or circumstance, shall be held invalid, the remainder of this Act, or the application of such provision to persons or circumstances other than those as to which it is held invalid, shall not be affected thereby.

# LABOR–MANAGEMENT REPORTING
# AND DISCLOSURE ACT *

73 Stat. 519 (1959), as amended, 29 U.S.C. §§ 401–531 (1982).

## AN ACT

To provide for the reporting and disclosure of certain financial transactions and administrative practices of labor organizations and employers, to prevent abuses in the administration of trusteeships by labor organizations, to provide standards with respect to the election of officers of labor organizations and for other purposes.

## SHORT TITLE

**Sec. 1.** This Act may be cited as the "Labor-Management Reporting and Disclosure Act of 1959".

## DECLARATION OF FINDINGS, PURPOSES, AND POLICY

**Sec. 2.** (a) The Congress finds that, in the public interest, it continues to be the responsibility of the Federal Government to protect employees' rights to organize, choose their own representatives, bargain collectively, and otherwise engage in concerted activities for their mutual aid or protection; that the relations between employers and labor organizations and the millions of workers they represent have a substantial impact on the commerce of the Nation; and that in order to accomplish the objective of a free flow of commerce it is essential that labor organizations, employers, and their officials adhere to the highest standards of responsibility and ethical conduct in administering the affairs of their organizations, particularly as they affect labor-management relations.

(b) The Congress further finds, from recent investigations in the labor and management fields, that there have been a number of instances of breach of trust, corruption, disregard of the rights of individual employees, and other failures to observe high standards of responsibility and ethical conduct which require further and supplementary legislation that will afford necessary protection of the rights and interests of employees and the public generally as they relate to the activities of labor organizations, employers, labor relations consultants, and their officers and representatives.

(c) The Congress, therefore, further finds and declares that the enactment of this Act is necessary to eliminate or prevent improper practices on the part of labor organizations, employers, labor relations consultants, and their officers and representatives which distort and defeat the policies of the Labor Management Relations Act, 1947, as

---

* Sections 201(d) and (e), Section 505, and all of Title VII of the LMRDA amend the NLRA and the LMRA and
are, accordingly, omitted here. They have been incorporated in the pertinent sections of those statutes.

amended, and the Railway Labor Act, as amended, and have the tendency or necessary effect of burdening or obstructing commerce by (1) impairing the efficiency, safety, or operation of the instrumentalities of commerce; (2) occurring in the current of commerce; (3) materially affecting, restraining, or controlling the flow of raw materials or manufactured or processed goods into or from the channels of commerce, or the prices of such materials or goods in commerce; or (4) causing diminution of employment and wages in such volume as substantially to impair or disrupt the market for goods flowing into or from the channels of commerce.

## DEFINITIONS

**Sec. 3.** For the purposes of titles I, II, III, IV, V (except section 505), and VI of this Act—

(a) "Commerce" means trade, traffic, commerce, transportation, transmission, or communication among the several States or between any State and any place outside thereof.

(b) "State" includes any State of the United States, the District of Columbia, Puerto Rico, the Virgin Islands, American Samoa, Guam, Wake Island, the Canal Zone, and Outer Continental Shelf lands defined in the Outer Continental Shelf Lands Act (43 U.S.C. 1331–1343).

(ç) "Industry affecting commerce" means any activity, business, or industry in commerce or in which a labor dispute would hinder or obstruct commerce or the free flow of commerce and includes any activity or industry "affecting commerce" within the meaning of the Labor Management Relations Act, 1947, as amended, or the Railway Labor Act, as amended.

(d) "Person" includes one or more individuals, labor organizations, partnerships, associations, corporations, legal representatives, mutual companies, joint-stock companies, trusts, unincorporated organizations, trustees, trustees in cases under title 11 of the United States Code, or receivers.

(e) "Employer" means any employer or any group or association of employers engaged in an industry affecting commerce (1) which is, with respect to employees engaged in an industry affecting commerce, an employer within the meaning of any law of the United States relating to the employment of any employees or (2) which may deal with any labor organization concerning grievances, labor disputes, wages, rates of pay, hours of employment, or conditions of work, and includes any person acting directly or indirectly as an employer or as an agent of an employer in relation to an employee but does not include the United States or any corporation wholly owned by the Government of the United States or any State or political subdivision thereof.

(f) "Employee" means any individual employed by an employer, and includes any individual whose work has ceased as a consequence of, or in connection with, any current labor dispute or because of any unfair labor practice or because of exclusion or expulsion from a labor organization in any manner or for any reason inconsistent with the requirements of this Act.

(g) "Labor dispute" includes any controversy concerning terms, tenure, or conditions of employment, or concerning the association or representation of persons in negotiating, fixing, maintaining, changing, or seeking to arrange terms or conditions of employment, regardless of whether the disputants stand in the proximate relation of employer and employee.

(h) "Trusteeship" means any receivership, trusteeship, or other method of supervision or control whereby a labor organization suspends the autonomy otherwise available to a subordinate body under its constitution or bylaws.

(i) "Labor organization" means a labor organization engaged in an industry affecting commerce and includes any organization of any kind, any agency, or employee representation committee, group, association, or plan so engaged in which employees participate and which exists for the purpose, in whole or in part, of dealing with employers concerning grievances, labor disputes, wages, rates of pay, hours, or other terms or conditions of employment, and any conference, general committee, joint or system board, or joint council so engaged which is subordinate to a national or international labor organization, other than a State or local central body.

(j) A labor organization shall be deemed to be engaged in an industry affecting commerce if it—

(1) is the certified representative of employees under the provisions of the National Labor Relations Act, as amended, or the Railway Labor Act, as amended; or

(2) although not certified, is a national or international labor organization or a local labor organization recognized or acting as the representative of employees of an employer or employers engaged in an industry affecting commerce; or

(3) has chartered a local labor organization or subsidiary body which is representing or actively seeking to represent employees of employers within the meaning of paragraph (1) or (2); or

(4) has been chartered by a labor organization representing or actively seeking to represent employees within the meaning of paragraph (1) or (2) as the local or subordinate body through which such employees may enjoy membership or become affiliated with such labor organization; or

(5) is a conference, general committee, joint or system board, or joint council, subordinate to a national or international labor organization, which includes a labor organization engaged in an industry affecting commerce within the meaning of any of the preceding paragraphs of this subsection, other than a State or local central body.

(k) "Secret ballot" means the expression by ballot, voting machine, or otherwise, but in no event by proxy, of a choice with respect to any election or vote taken upon any matter, which is cast in such a manner that the person expressing such choice cannot be identified with the choice expressed.

(*l*) "Trust in which a labor organization is interested" means a trust or other fund or organization (1) which was created or established by a labor organization, or one or more of the trustees or one or more members of the governing body of which is selected or appointed by a labor organization, and (2) a primary purpose of which is to provide benefits for the members of such labor organization or their beneficiaries.

(m) "Labor relations consultant" means any person who, for compensation, advises or represents an employer, employer organization, or labor organization concerning employee organizing, concerted activities, or collective bargaining activities.

(n) "Officer" means any constitutional officer, any person authorized to perform the functions of president, vice president, secretary, treasurer, or other executive functions of a labor organization, and any member of its executive board or similar governing body.

(o) "Member" or "member in good standing", when used in reference to a labor organization, includes any person who has fulfilled the requirements for membership in such organization, and who neither has voluntarily withdrawn from membership nor has been expelled or suspended from membership after appropriate proceedings consistent with lawful provisions of the constitution and bylaws of such organization.

(p) "Secretary" means the Secretary of Labor.

(q) "Officer, agent, shop steward, or other representative", when used with respect to a labor organization, includes elected officials and key administrative personnel, whether elected or appointed (such as business agents, heads of departments or major units, and organizers who exercise substantial independent authority), but does not include salaried nonsupervisory professional staff, stenographic, and service personnel.

(r) "District court of the United States" means a United States district court and a United States court of any place subject to the jurisdiction of the United States.

# TITLE I—BILL OF RIGHTS OF MEMBERS OF LABOR ORGANIZATIONS

BILL OF RIGHTS

**Sec. 101.** **(a)(1) Equal Rights.**—Every member of a labor organization shall have equal rights and privileges within such organization to nominate candidates, to vote in elections or referendums of the labor organization, to attend membership meetings, and to participate in the deliberations and voting upon the business of such meetings, subject to reasonable rules and regulations in such organization's constitution and bylaws.

**(2) Freedom of Speech and Assembly.**—Every member of any labor organization shall have the right to meet and assemble freely with other members; and to express any views, arguments, or opinions; and to express at meetings of the labor organization his views, upon candidates in an election of the labor organization or upon any business properly before the meeting, subject to the organization's established and reasonable rules pertaining to the conduct of meetings: *Provided,* That nothing herein shall be construed to impair the right of a labor organization to adopt and enforce reasonable rules as to the responsibility of every member toward the organization as an institution and to his refraining from conduct that would interfere with its performance of its legal or contractual obligations.

**(3) Dues, Initiation Fees, and Assessments.**—Except in the case of a federation of national or international labor organizations, the rates of dues and initiation fees payable by members of any labor organization in effect on the date of enactment of this Act shall not be increased, and no general or special assessment shall be levied upon such members, except—

(A) in the case of a local labor organization, (i) by majority vote by secret ballot of the members in good standing voting at a general or special membership meeting, after reasonable notice of the intention to vote upon such question, or (ii) by majority vote of the members in good standing voting in a membership referendum conducted by secret ballot; or

(B) in the case of a labor organization, other than a local labor organization or a federation of national or international labor organizations, (i) by majority vote of the delegates voting at a regular convention, or at a special convention of such labor organization held upon not less than thirty days' written notice to the principal office of each local or constituent labor organization entitled to such notice, or (ii) by majority vote of the members in good standing of such labor organization voting in a membership referendum conducted by secret ballot, or (iii) by majority vote of the members of the executive board or similar govern-

ing body of such labor organization, pursuant to express authority contained in the constitution and bylaws of such labor organization: *Provided,* That such action on the part of the executive
board or similar governing body shall be effective only until the
next regular convention of such labor organization.

**(4) Protection of the Right To Sue.**—No labor organization shall
limit the right of any member thereof to institute an action in any
court, or in a proceeding before any administrative agency, irrespective
of whether or not the labor organization or its officers are named as defendants or respondents in such action or proceeding, or the right of
any member of a labor organization to appear as a witness in any judicial, administrative, or legislative proceeding, or to petition any legisla-
ture or to communicate with any legislator: *Provided,* That any such
member may be required to exhaust reasonable hearing procedures
(but not to exceed a four-month lapse of time) within such organization, before instituting legal or administrative proceedings against such
organizations or any officer thereof: *And provided further,* That no interested employer or employer association shall directly or indirectly
finance, encourage, or participate in, except as a party, any such action, proceeding, appearance, or petition.

**(5) Safeguards Against Improper Disciplinary Action.**—No member of any labor organization may be fined, suspended, expelled, or
otherwise disciplined except for nonpayment of dues by such organization or by any officer thereof unless such member has been (A)
served with written specific charges; (B) given a reasonable time to
prepare his defense; (C) afforded a full and fair hearing.

(b) Any provision of the constitution and bylaws of any labor organization which is inconsistent with the provisions of this section
shall be of no force or effect.

## CIVIL ENFORCEMENT

**Sec. 102.** Any person whose rights secured by the provisions of
this title have been infringed by any violation of this title may bring a
civil action in a district court of the United States for such relief (including injunctions) as may be appropriate. Any such action against
a labor organization shall be brought in the district court of the United
States for the district where the alleged violation occurred, or where
the principal office of such labor organization is located.

## RETENTION OF EXISTING RIGHTS

**Sec. 103.** Nothing contained in this title shall limit the rights
and remedies of any member of a labor organization under any State
or Federal law or before any court or other tribunal, or under the constitution and bylaws of any labor organization.

RIGHT TO COPIES OF COLLECTIVE BARGAINING AGREEMENTS

**Sec. 104.** It shall be the duty of the secretary or corresponding principal officer of each labor organization, in the case of a local labor organization, to forward a copy of each collective bargaining agreement made by such labor organization with any employer to any employee who requests such a copy and whose rights as such employee are directly affected by such agreement, and in the case of a labor organization other than a local labor organization, to forward a copy of any such agreement to each constituent unit which has members directly affected by such agreement; and such officer shall maintain at the principal office of the labor organization of which he is an officer copies of any such agreement made or received by such labor organization, which copies shall be available for inspection by any member or by any employee whose rights are affected by such agreement. The provisions of section 210 shall be applicable in the enforcement of this section.

INFORMATION AS TO ACT

**Sec. 105.** Every labor organization shall inform its members concerning the provisions of this Act.

## TITLE II—REPORTING BY LABOR ORGANIZATIONS, OFFICERS AND EMPLOYEES OF LABOR ORGANIZATIONS, AND EMPLOYERS

REPORT OF LABOR ORGANIZATIONS

**Sec. 201.** (a) Every labor organization shall adopt a constitution and bylaws and shall file a copy thereof with the Secretary, together with a report, signed by its president and secretary or corresponding principal officers, containing the following information—

(1) the name of the labor organization, its mailing address, and any other address at which it maintains its principal office or at which it keeps the records referred to in this title;

(2) the name and title of each of its officers;

(3) the initiation fee or fees required from a new or transferred member and fees for work permits required by the reporting labor organization;

(4) the regular dues or fees or other periodic payments required to remain a member of the reporting labor organization; and

(5) detailed statements, or references to specific provisions of documents filed under this subsection which contain such statements, showing the provision made and procedures followed with respect to each of the following: (A) qualifications for or restric-

tions on membership, (B) levying of assessments, (C) participation in insurance or other benefit plans, (D) authorization for disbursement of funds of the labor organization, (E) audit of financial transactions of the labor organization, (F) the calling of regular and special meetings, (G) the selection of officers and stewards and of any representatives to other bodies composed of labor organizations' representatives, with a specific statement of the manner in which each officer was elected, appointed, or otherwise selected, (H) discipline or removal of officers or agents for breaches of their trust, (I) imposition of fines, suspensions, and expulsions of members, including the grounds for such action and any provision made for notice, hearing, judgment on the evidence, and appeal procedures, (J) authorization for bargaining demands, (K) ratification of contract terms, (L) authorization for strikes, and (M) issuance of work permits. Any change in the information required by this subsection shall be reported to the Secretary at the time the reporting labor organization files with the Secretary the annual financial report required by subsection (b).

(b) Every labor organization shall file annually with the Secretary a financial report signed by its president and treasurer or corresponding principal officers containing the following information in such detail as may be necessary accurately to disclose its financial condition and operations for its preceding fiscal year—

(1) assets and liabilities at the beginning and end of the fiscal year;

(2) receipts of any kind and the sources thereof;

(3) salary, allowances, and other direct or indirect disbursements (including reimbursed expenses) to each officer and also to each employee who, during such fiscal year, received more than $10,000 in the aggregate from such labor organization and any other labor organization affiliated with it or with which it is affiliated, or which is affiliated with the same national or international labor organization;

(4) direct and indirect loans made to any officer, employee, or member, which aggregated more than $250 during the fiscal year, together with a statement of the purpose, security, if any, and arrangements for repayment;

(5) direct and indirect loans to any business enterprise, together with a statement of the purpose, security, if any, and arrangements for repayment; and

(6) other disbursements made by it including the purposes thereof; all in such categories as the Secretary may prescribe.

(c) Every labor organization required to submit a report under this title shall make available the information required to be contained in such report to all of its members, and every such labor organization and its officers shall be under a duty enforceable at the suit of any member of such organization in any State court of competent jurisdiction or in the district court of the United States for the district in which such labor organization maintains its principal office, to permit such member for just cause to examine any books, records, and accounts necessary to verify such report. The court in such action may, in its discretion, in addition to any judgment awarded to the plaintiff or plaintiffs, allow a reasonable attorney's fee to be paid by the defendant, and costs of the action.

## REPORT OF OFFICERS AND EMPLOYEES OF LABOR ORGANIZATIONS

**Sec. 202.** (a) Every officer of a labor organization and every employee of a labor organization (other than an employee performing exclusively clerical or custodial services) shall file with the Secretary a signed report listing and describing for his preceding fiscal year—

(1) any stock, bond, security, or other interest, legal or equitable, which he or his spouse or minor child directly or indirectly held in, and any income or any other benefit with monetary value (including reimbursed expenses) which he or his spouse or minor child derived directly or indirectly from, an employer whose employees such labor organization represents or is actively seeking to represent, except payments and other benefits received as a bona fide employee of such employer;

(2) any transaction in which he or his spouse or minor child engaged, directly or indirectly, involving any stock, bond, security, or loan to or from, or other legal or equitable interest in the business of an employer whose employees such labor organization represents or is actively seeking to represent;

(3) any stock, bond, security, or other interest, legal or equitable, which he or his spouse or minor child directly or indirectly held in, and any income or any other benefit with monetary value (including reimbursed expenses) which he or his spouse or minor child directly or indirectly derived from, any business a substantial part of which consists of buying from, selling or leasing to, or otherwise dealing with, the business of an employer whose employees such labor organization represents or is actively seeking to represent;

(4) any stock, bond, security, or other interest, legal or equitable, which he or his spouse or minor child directly or indirectly held in, and any income or any other benefit with monetary value (including reimbursed expenses) which he or his spouse or minor child directly or indirectly derived from, a business any part of which consists of buying from, or selling or leasing directly or indirectly to, or otherwise dealing with such labor organization;

(5) any direct or indirect business transaction or arrangement between him or his spouse or minor child and any employer whose employees his organization represents or is actively seeking to represent, except work performed and payments and benefits received as a bona fide employee of such employer and except purchases and sales of goods or services in the regular course of business at prices generally available to any employee of such employer; and

(6) any payment of money or other thing of value (including reimbursed expenses) which he or his spouse or minor child received directly or indirectly from any employer or any person who acts as a labor relations consultant to an employer, except payments of the kinds referred to in section 302(c) of the Labor Management Relations Act, 1947, as amended.

(b) The provisions of paragraphs (1), (2), (3), (4), and (5) of subsection (a) shall not be construed to require any such officer or employee to report his bona fide investments in securities traded on a securities exchange registered as a national securities exchange under the Securities Exchange Act of 1934, in shares in an investment company registered under the Investment Company Act of 1940, or in securities of a public utility holding company registered under the Public Utility Holding Company Act of 1935, or to report any income derived therefrom.

(c) Nothing contained in this section shall be construed to require any officer or employee of a labor organization to file a report under subsection (a) unless he or his spouse or minor child holds or has held an interest, has received income or any other benefit with monetary value or a loan, or has engaged in a transaction described therein.

## REPORT OF EMPLOYERS

Sec. 203. (a) Every employer who in any fiscal year made—

(1) any payment or loan, direct or indirect, of money or other thing of value (including reimbursed expenses), or any promise or agreement therefor, to any labor organization or officer, agent, shop steward, or other representative of a labor organization, or employee of any labor organization, except (A) payments or loans made by any national or State bank, credit union, insurance company, savings and loan association or other credit institution and (B) payments of the kind referred to in section 302(c) of the Labor Management Relations Act, 1947, as amended;

(2) any payment (including reimbursed expenses) to any of his employees, or any group or committee of such employees, for the purpose of causing such employee or group or committee of employees to persuade other employees to exercise or not to exercise, or as the manner of exercising, the right to organize and

bargain collectively through representatives of their own choosing unless such payments were contemporaneously or previously disclosed to such other employees;

(3) any expenditure, during the fiscal year, where an object thereof, directly or indirectly, is to interfere with, restrain, or coerce employees in the exercise of the right to organize and bargain collectively through representatives of their own choosing, or is to obtain information concerning the activities of employees or a labor organization in connection with a labor dispute involving such employer, except for use solely in conjunction with an administrative or arbitral proceeding or a criminal or civil judicial proceeding;

(4) any agreement or arrangement with a labor relations consultant or other independent contractor or organization pursuant to which such person undertakes activities where an object thereof, directly or indirectly, is to persuade employees to exercise or not to exercise, or persuade employees as to the manner of exercising, the right to organize and bargain collectively through representatives of their own choosing, or undertakes to supply such employer with information concerning the activities of employees or a labor organization in connection with a labor dispute involving such employer, except information for use solely in conjunction with an administrative or arbitral proceeding or a criminal or civil judicial proceeding; or

(5) any payment (including reimbursed expenses) pursuant to an agreement or arrangement described in subdivision (4);

shall file with the Secretary a report, in a form prescribed by him, signed by its president and treasurer or corresponding principal officers showing in detail the date and amount of each such payment, loan, promise, agreement, or arrangement and the name, address, and position, if any, in any firm or labor organization of the person to whom it was made and a full explanation of the circumstances of all such payments, including the terms of any agreement or understanding pursuant to which they were made.

(b) Every person who pursuant to any agreement or arrangement with an employer undertakes activities where an object thereof is, directly or indirectly—

(1) to persuade employees to exercise or not to exercise, or persuade employees as to the manner of exercising, the right to organize and bargain collectively through representatives of their own choosing; or

(2) to supply an employer with information concerning the activities of employees or a labor organization in connection with a labor dispute involving such employer, except information for use solely in conjunction with an administrative or arbitral proceeding or a criminal or civil judicial proceeding;

shall file within thirty days after entering into such agreement or arrangement a report with the Secretary, signed by its president and treasurer or corresponding principal officers, containing the name under which such person is engaged in doing business and the address of its principal office, and a detailed statement of the terms and conditions of such agreement or arrangement. Every such person shall file annually, with respect to each fiscal year during which payments were made as a result of such an agreement or arrangement, a report with the Secretary, signed by its president and treasurer or corresponding principal officers, containing a statement (A) of its receipts of any kind from employers on account of labor relations advice or services, designating the sources thereof, and (B) of its disbursements of any kind, in connection with such services and the purposes thereof. In each such case such information shall be set forth in such categories as the Secretary may prescribe.

(c) Nothing in this section shall be construed to require any employer or other person to file a report covering the services of such person by reason of his giving or agreeing to give advice to such employer or representing or agreeing to represent such employer before any court, administrative agency, or tribunal of arbitration or engaging or agreeing to engage in collective bargaining on behalf of such employer with respect to wages, hours, or other terms or conditions of employment or the negotiation of an agreement or any question arising thereunder.

(d) Nothing contained in this section shall be construed to require an employer to file a report under subsection (a) unless he has made an expenditure, payment, loan, agreement, or arrangement of the kind described therein. Nothing contained in this section shall be construed to require any other person to file a report under subsection (b) unless he was a party to an agreement or arrangement of the kind described therein.

(e) Nothing contained in this section shall be construed to require any regular officer, supervisor, or employee of an employer to file a report in connection with services rendered to such employer nor shall any employer be required to file a report covering expenditures made to any regular officer, supervisor, or employee of an employer as compensation for service as a regular officer, supervisor, or employee of such employer.

(f) Nothing contained in this section shall be construed as an amendment to, or modification of the rights protected by, section 8(c) of the National Labor Relations Act, as amended.

(g) The term "interfere with, restrain, or coerce" as used in this section means interference, restraint, and coercion which, if done with respect to the exercise of rights guaranteed in section 7 of the National Labor Relations Act, as amended, would, under section 8(a) of such Act, constitute an unfair labor practice.

## ATTORNEY-CLIENT COMMUNICATIONS EXEMPTED

**Sec. 204.** Nothing contained in this Act shall be construed to require an attorney who is a member in good standing of the bar of any State, to include in any report required to be filed pursuant to the provisions of this Act any information which was lawfully communicated to such attorney by any of his clients in the course of a legitimate attorney-client relationship.

## REPORTS MADE PUBLIC INFORMATION

**Sec. 205.** (a) The contents of the reports and documents filed with the Secretary pursuant to sections 201, 202, 203, and 211 shall be public information, and the Secretary may publish any information and data which he obtains pursuant to the provisions of this title. The Secretary may use the information and data for statistical and research purposes, and compile and publish such studies, analyses, reports, and surveys based thereon as he may deem appropriate.

(b) The Secretary shall by regulation make reasonable provision for the inspection and examination, on the request of any person, of the information and data contained in any report or other document filed with him pursuant to sections 201, 202, 203, or 211.

(c) The Secretary shall by regulation provide for the furnishing by the Department of Labor of copies of reports or other documents filed with the Secretary pursuant to this title, upon payment of a charge based upon the cost of the service. The Secretary shall make available without payment of a charge, or require any person to furnish, to such State agency as is designated by law or by the Governor of the State in which such person has his principal place of business or headquarters, upon request of the Governor of such State, copies of any reports and documents filed by such person with the Secretary pursuant to section 201, 202, 203, or 211, or of information and data contained therein. No person shall be required by reason of any law of any State to furnish to any officer or agency of such State any information included in a report filed by such person with the Secretary pursuant to the provisions of this title, if a copy of such report, or of the portion thereof containing such information, is furnished to such officer or agency. All moneys received in payment of such charges fixed by the Secretary pursuant to this subsection shall be deposited in the general fund of the Treasury.

## RETENTION OF RECORDS

**Sec. 206.** Every person required to file any report under this title shall maintain records on the matters required to be reported which will provide in sufficient detail the necessary basic information and data from which the documents filed with the Secretary may be verified, explained or clarified, and checked for accuracy and completeness, and shall include vouchers, worksheets, receipts, and applicable resolutions, and shall keep such records available for examination for a period of not less than five years after the filing of the documents based on the information which they contain.

## EFFECTIVE DATE

**Sec. 207.** (a) Each labor organization shall file the initial report required under section 201(a) within ninety days after the date on which it first becomes subject to this Act.

(b) Each person required to file a report under section 201(b), 202, 203(a), the second sentence of 203(b), or section 211, shall file such report within ninety days after the end of each of its fiscal years; except that where such person is subject to section 201(b), 202, 203(a), the second sentence of 203(b), or section 211, as the case may be, for only a portion of such a fiscal year (because the date of enactment of this Act occurs during such person's fiscal year or such person becomes subject to this Act during its fiscal year) such person may consider that portion as the entire fiscal year in making such report.

## RULES AND REGULATIONS

**Sec. 208.** The Secretary shall have authority to issue, amend, and rescind rules and regulations prescribing the form and publication of reports required to be filed under this title and such other reasonable rules and regulations (including rules prescribing reports concerning trusts in which a labor organization is interested) as he may find necessary to prevent the circumvention or evasion of such reporting requirements. In exercising his power under this section the Secretary shall prescribe by general rule simplified reports for labor organizations or employers for whom he finds that by virtue of their size a detailed report would be unduly burdensome, but the Secretary may revoke such provision for simplified forms of any labor organization or employer if he determines, after such investigation as he deems proper and due notice and opportunity for a hearing, that the purposes of this section would be served thereby.

## CRIMINAL PROVISIONS

**Sec. 209.** (a) Any person who willfully violates this title shall be fined not more than $10,000 or imprisoned for not more than one year, or both.

(b) Any person who makes a false statement or representation of a material fact, knowing it to be false, or who knowingly fails to disclose a material fact, in any document, report, or other information required under the provisions of this title shall be fined not more than $10,000 or imprisoned for not more than one year, or both.

(c) Any person who willfully makes a false entry in or willfully conceals, withholds, or destroys any books, records, reports, or statements required to be kept by any provision of this title shall be fined not more than $10,000 or imprisoned for not more than one year, or both.

(d) Each individual required to sign reports under sections 201 and 203 shall be personally responsible for the filing of such reports and for any statement contained therein which he knows to be false.

### CIVIL ENFORCEMENT

**Sec. 210.** Whenever it shall appear that any person has violated or is about to violate any of the provisions of this title, the Secretary may bring a civil action for such relief (including injunctions) as may be appropriate. Any such action may be brought in the district court of the United States where the violation occurred or, at the option of the parties, in the United States District Court for the District of Columbia.

### SURETY COMPANY REPORTS

**Sec. 211.** Each surety company which issues any bond required by this Act or the Employment Retirement Income Security Act of 1974 shall file annually with the Secretary, with respect to each fiscal year during which any such bond was in force, a report, in such form and detail as he may prescribe by regulation, filed by the president and treasurer or corresponding principal officers of the surety company, describing its bond experience under each such Act, including information as to the premiums received, total claims paid, amounts recovered by way of subrogation, administrative and legal expenses and such related data and information as the Secretary shall determine to be necessary in the public interest and to carry out the policy of the Act. Notwithstanding the foregoing, if the Secretary finds that any such specific information cannot be practicably ascertained or would be uninformative, the Secretary may modify or waive the requirement for such information.

## TITLE III—TRUSTEESHIPS

### REPORTS

**Sec. 301.** (a) Every labor organization which has or assumes trusteeship over any subordinate labor organization shall file with the Secretary within thirty days after the date of the enactment of this Act or the imposition of any such trusteeship, and semiannually thereafter, a report, signed by its president and treasurer or corresponding principal officers, as well as by the trustees of such subordinate labor organization, containing the following information: (1) the name and address of the subordinate organization; (2) the date of establishing the trusteeship; (3) a detailed statement of the reason or reasons for establishing or continuing the trusteeship; and (4) the nature and extent of participation by the membership of the subordinate organization in the selection of delegates to represent such organization in regular or special conventions or other policy-determining bodies and in the election of officers of the labor organization which has assumed trusteeship over such subordinate organization. The initial report shall also include a full and complete account of the financial condition of such subordinate organization as of the time trusteeship was assumed over it. During the continuance of a trusteeship the labor organization which has assumed trusteeship over a subordinate labor organization shall file on behalf of the subordinate labor organization the annual financial report required by section 201 (b) signed by the president and treasurer or corresponding principal officers of the labor organization which has assumed such trusteeship and the trustees of the subordinate labor organization.

(b) The provisions of sections 201(c), 205, 206, 208, and 210 shall be applicable to reports filed under this title.

(c) Any person who willfully violates this section shall be fined not more than $10,000 or imprisoned for not more than one year, or both.

(d) Any person who makes a false statement or representation of a material fact, knowing it to be false, or who knowingly fails to disclose a material fact, in any report required under the provisions of this section or willfully makes any false entry in or willfully withholds, conceals, or destroys any documents, books, records, reports, or statements upon which such report is based, shall be fined not more than $10,000 or imprisoned for not more than one year, or both.

(e) Each individual required to sign a report under this section shall be personally responsible for the filing of such report and for any statement contained therein which he knows to be false.

### PURPOSES FOR WHICH A TRUSTEESHIP MAY BE ESTABLISHED

**Sec. 302.** Trusteeships shall be established and administered by a labor organization over a subordinate body only in accordance with the constitution and bylaws of the organization which has assumed trusteeship over the subordinate body and for the purpose of correcting corruption or financial malpractice, assuring the performance of collective bargaining agreements or other duties of a bargaining representative, restoring democratic procedures, or otherwise carrying out the legitimate objects of such labor organization.

### UNLAWFUL ACTS RELATING TO LABOR ORGANIZATION UNDER TRUSTEESHIP

**Sec. 303.** (a) During any period when a subordinate body of a labor organization is in trusteeship, it shall be unlawful (1) to count the vote of delegates from such body in any convention or election of officers of the labor organization unless the delegates have been chosen by secret ballot in an election in which all the members in good standing of such subordinate body were eligible to participate, or (2) to transfer to such organization any current receipts or other funds of the subordinate body except the normal per capita tax and assessments payable by subordinate bodies not in trusteeship: *Provided,* That nothing herein contained shall prevent the distribution of the assets of a labor organization in accordance with its constitution and bylaws upon the bona fide dissolution thereof.

(b) Any person who willfully violates this section shall be fined not more than $10,000 or imprisoned for not more than one year, or both.

ENFORCEMENT

**Sec. 304.** (a) Upon the written complaint of any member or subordinate body of a labor organization alleging that such organization has violated the provisions of this title (except section 301) the Secretary shall investigate the complaint and if the Secretary finds probable cause to believe that such violation has occurred and has not been remedied he shall, without disclosing the identity of the complainant, bring a civil action in any district court of the United States having jurisdiction of the labor organization for such relief (including injunctions) as may be appropriate. Any member or subordinate body of a labor organization affected by any violation of this title (except section 301) may bring a civil action in any district court of the United States having jurisdiction of the labor organization for such relief (including injunctions) as may be appropriate.

(b) For the purpose of actions under this section, district courts of the United States shall be deemed to have jurisdiction of a labor organization (1) in the district in which the principal office of such labor organization is located, or (2) in any district in which its duly authorized officers or agents are engaged in conducting the affairs of the trusteeship.

(c) In any proceeding pursuant to this section a trusteeship established by a labor organization in conformity with the procedural requirements of its constitution and bylaws and authorized or ratified after a fair hearing either before the executive board or before such other body as may be provided in accordance with its constitution or bylaws shall be presumed valid for a period of eighteen months from the date of its establishment and shall not be subject to attack during such period except upon clear and convincing proof that the trusteeship was not established or maintained in good faith for a purpose allowable under section 302. After the expiration of eighteen months the trusteeship shall be presumed invalid in any such proceeding and its discontinuance shall be decreed unless the labor organization shall show by clear and convincing proof that the continuation of the trusteeship is necessary for a purpose allowable under section 302. In the latter event the court may dismiss the complaint or retain jurisdiction of the cause on such conditions and for such period as it deems appropriate.

## REPORT TO CONGRESS

**Sec. 305.** The Secretary shall submit to the Congress at the expiration of three years from the date of enactment of this Act a report upon the operation of this title.

## COMPLAINT BY SECRETARY

**Sec. 306.** The rights and remedies provided by this title shall be in addition to any and all other rights and remedies at law or in equity: *Provided,* That upon the filing of a complaint by the Secretary the jurisdiction of the district court over such trusteeship shall be exclusive and the final judgment shall be res judicata.

## TITLE IV—ELECTIONS

### TERMS OF OFFICE; ELECTION PROCEDURES

**Sec. 401.** (a) Every national or international labor organization, except a federation of national or international labor organizations, shall elect its officers not less often than once every five years either by secret ballot among the members in good standing or at a convention of delegates chosen by secret ballot.

(b) Every local labor organization shall elect its officers not less often than once every three years by secret ballot among the members in good standing.

(c) Every national or international labor organization, except a federation of national or international labor organizations, and every local labor organization, and its officers, shall be under a duty, enforceable at the suit of any bona fide candidate for office in such labor organization in the district court of the United States in which such labor organization maintains its principal office, to comply with all reasonable requests of any candidate to distribute by mail or otherwise at the candidate's expense campaign literature in aid of such person's candidacy to all members in good standing of such labor organization and to refrain from discrimination in favor of or against any candidate with respect to the use of lists of members, and whenever such labor organizations or its officers authorize the distribution by mail or otherwise to members of campaign literature on behalf of any candidate or of the labor organization itself with reference to such election, similar distribution at the request of any other bona fide candidate shall be made by such labor organization and its officers, with equal treatment as to the expense of such distribution. Every bona fide candidate shall have the right, once within 30 days prior to an election of a labor organization in which he is a candidate, to inspect a list containing the names and last known addresses of all members of the labor organization who are subject to a collective bargaining agreement requiring membership therein as a condition of employment, which list shall be maintained and kept at the principal office of such labor organization by a designated official thereof. Adequate safeguards to insure a fair election shall be provided, including the right of any candidate to have an observer at the polls and at the counting of the ballots.

(d) Officers of intermediate bodies, such as general committees, system boards, joint boards, or joint councils, shall be elected not less often than once every four years by secret ballot among the members in good standing or by labor organization officers representative of such members who have been elected by secret ballot.

(e) In any election required by this section which is to be held by secret ballot a reasonable opportunity shall be given for the nomination of candidates and every member in good standing shall be eligible to be a candidate and to hold office (subject to section 504 and to reasonable qualifications uniformly imposed) and shall have the right to vote for or otherwise support the candidate or candidates of his choice, without being subject to penalty, discipline, or improper interference or reprisal of any kind by such organization or any member thereof. Not less than fifteen days prior to the election notice thereof shall be mailed to each member at his last known home address. Each member in good standing shall be entitled to one vote. No member whose dues have been withheld by his employer for payment to such organization pursuant to his voluntary authorization provided for in a collective bargaining agreement shall be declared ineligible to vote or be a candidate for office in such organization by reason of alleged delay or default in the payment of dues. The votes cast by members of each local labor organization shall be counted, and the results published, separately. The election officials designated in the constitution and bylaws or the secretary, if no other official is designated, shall preserve for one year the ballots and all other records pertaining to the election. The election shall be conducted in accordance with the constitution and bylaws of such organization insofar as they are not inconsistent with the provisions of this title.

(f) When officers are chosen by a convention of delegates elected by secret ballot, the convention shall be conducted in accordance with the constitution and bylaws of the labor organization insofar as they are not inconsistent with the provisions of this title. The officials designated in the constitution and bylaws or the secretary, if no other is designated, shall preserve for one year the credentials of the delegates and all minutes and other records of the convention pertaining to the election of officers.

(g) No moneys received by any labor organization by way of dues, assessment, or similar levy, and no moneys of an employer shall be contributed or applied to promote the candidacy of any person in an election subject to the provisions of this title. Such moneys of a labor organization may be utilized for notices, factual statements of issues not involving candidates, and other expenses necessary for the holding of an election.

(h) If the Secretary, upon application of any member of a local labor organization, finds after hearing in accordance with the Administrative Procedure Act that the constitution and bylaws of such labor organization do not provide an adequate procedure for the removal of an elected officer guilty of serious misconduct, such officer may be removed, for cause shown and after notice and hearing, by the members in good standing voting in a secret ballot conducted by the officers of such labor organization in accordance with its constitution and bylaws insofar as they are not inconsistent with the provisions of this title.

(i) The Secretary shall promulgate rules and regulations prescribing minimum standards and procedures for determining the adequacy of the removal procedures to which reference is made in subsection (h).

### Enforcement

**Sec. 402.** (a) A member of a labor organization—

(1) who has exhausted the remedies available under the constitution and bylaws of such organization and of any parent body, or

(2) who has invoked such available remedies without obtaining a final decision within three calendar months after their invocation,

may file a complaint with the Secretary within one calendar month thereafter alleging the violation of any provision of section 401 (including violation of the constitution and bylaws of the labor organization pertaining to the election and removal of officers). The challenged election shall be presumed valid pending a final decision thereon (as hereinafter provided) and in the interim the affairs of the organization shall be conducted by the officers elected or in such other manner as its constitution and bylaws may provide.

(b) The Secretary shall investigate such complaint and, if he finds probable cause to believe that a violation of this title has occurred and has not been remedied, he shall, within sixty days after the filing of such complaint, bring a civil action against the labor organization as an entity in the district court of the United States in which such labor organization maintains its principal office to set aside the invalid election, if any, and to direct the conduct of an election or hearing and vote upon the removal of officers under the supervision of the Secretary and in accordance with the provisions of this title and such rules and regulations as the Secretary may prescribe. The court shall have power to take such action as it deems proper to preserve the assets of the labor organization.

(c) If, upon a preponderance of the evidence after a trial upon the merits, the court finds—

(1) that an election has not been held within the time prescribed by section 401, or

(2) that the violation of section 401 may have affected the outcome of an election,

that court shall declare the election, if any, to be void and direct the conduct of a new election under supervision of the Secretary and, so far as lawful and practicable, in conformity with the constitution and bylaws of the labor organization. The Secretary shall promptly certify to the court the names of the persons elected, and the court shall thereupon enter a decree declaring such persons to be the officers of the labor organization. If the proceeding is for the removal of officers pursuant to subsection (h) of section 401, the Secretary shall certify the results of the vote and the court shall enter a decree declaring whether such persons have been removed as officers of the labor organization.

(d) An order directing an election, dismissing a complaint, or designating elected officers of a labor organization shall be appealable in the same manner as the final judgment in a civil action, but an order directing an election shall not be stayed pending appeal.

## APPLICATION OF OTHER LAWS

**Sec. 403.** No labor organization shall be required by law to conduct elections of officers with greater frequency or in a different form or manner than is required by its own constitution or bylaws, except as otherwise provided by this title. Existing rights and remedies to enforce the constitution and bylaws of a labor organization with respect to elections prior to the conduct thereof shall not be affected by the provisions of this title. The remedy provided by this title for challenging an election already conducted shall be exclusive.

## EFFECTIVE DATE

**Sec. 404.** The provisions of this title shall become applicable—

(1) ninety days after the date of enactment of this Act in the case of a labor organization whose constitution and bylaws can lawfully be modified or amended by action of its constitutional officers or governing body, or

(2) where such modification can only be made by a constitutional convention of the labor organization, not later than the next constitutional convention of such labor organization after

the date of enactment of this Act, or one year after such date, whichever is sooner.  If no such convention is held within such one-year period, the executive board or similar governing body empowered to act for such labor organization between conventions is empowered to make such interim constitutional changes as are necessary to carry out the provisions of this title.

## TITLE V—SAFEGUARDS FOR LABOR ORGANIZATIONS

### FIDUCIARY RESPONSIBILITY OF OFFICERS OF LABOR ORGANIZATIONS

**Sec. 501.** (a) The officers, agents, shop stewards, and other representatives of a labor organization occupy positions of trust in relation to such organization and its members as a group.  It is, therefore, the duty of each such person, taking into account the special problems and functions of a labor organization, to hold its money and property solely for the benefit of the organization and its members and to manage, invest, and expend the same in accordance with its constitution and bylaws and any resolutions of the governing bodies adopted thereunder, to refrain from dealing with such organization as an adverse party or in behalf of an adverse party in any matter connected with his duties and from holding or acquiring any pecuniary or personal interest which conflicts with the interests of such organization, and to account to the organization for any profit received by him in whatever capacity in connection with transactions conducted by him or under his direction on behalf of the organization.  A general exculpatory provision in the constitution and bylaws of such a labor organization or a general exculpatory resolution of a governing body purporting to relieve any such person of liability for breach of the duties declared by this section shall be void as against public policy.

(b) When any officer, agent, shop steward, or representative of any labor organization is alleged to have violated the duties declared in subsection (a) and the labor organization or its governing board or officers refuse or fail to sue or recover damages or secure an accounting or other appropriate relief within a reasonable time after being requested to do so by any member of the labor organization, such member may sue such officer, agent, shop steward, or representative in any district court of the United States or in any State court of competent jurisdiction to recover damages or secure an accounting or other appropriate relief for the benefit of the labor organization.  No such proceeding shall be brought except upon leave of the court obtained upon verified application and for good cause shown, which application may be made ex parte.  The trial judge may allot a reasonable part of the recovery in any action under this subsection to pay the fees of counsel prosecuting the suit at the instance of the member of the labor organization and to compensate such member for any expenses necessarily paid or incurred by him in connection with the litigation.

(c) Any person who embezzles, steals, or unlawfully and willfully abstracts or converts to his own use, or the use of another, any of the moneys, funds, securities, property, or other assets of a labor organization of which he is an officer, or by which he is employed, directly or indirectly, shall be fined not more than $10,000 or imprisoned for not more than five years, or both.

## Bonding

**Sec. 502.** (a) Every officer, agent, shop steward, or other representative or employee of any labor organization (other than a labor organization whose property and annual financial receipts do not exceed $5,000 in value), or of a trust in which a labor organization is interested, who handles funds or other property thereof shall be bonded to provide protection against loss by reason of acts of fraud or dishonesty on his part directly or through connivance with others. The bond of each such person shall be fixed at the beginning of the organization's fiscal year and shall be in an amount not less than 10 per centum of the funds handled by him and his predecessor or predecessors, if any, during the preceding fiscal year, but in no case more than $500,000. If the labor organization or the trust in which a labor organization is interested does not have a preceding fiscal year, the amount of the bond shall be, in the case of a local labor organization, not less than $1,000, and in the case of any other labor organization or of a trust in which a labor organization is interested, not less than $10,000. Such bonds shall be individual or schedule in form, and shall have a corporate surety company as surety thereon. Any person who is not covered by such bonds shall not be permitted to receive, handle, disburse, or otherwise exercise custody or control of the funds or other property of a labor organization or of a trust in which a labor organization is interested. No such bond shall be placed through an agent or broker or with a surety company in which any labor organization or any officer, agent, shop steward, or other representative of a labor organization has any direct or indirect interest. Such surety company shall be a corporate surety which holds a grant of authority from the Secretary of the Treasury under the Act of July 30, 1947 (6 U.S.C. 6–13), as an acceptable surety on Federal bonds: *Provided,* That when in the opinion of the Secretary a labor organization has made other bonding arrangements which would provide the protection required by this section at comparable cost or less, he may exempt such labor organization from placing a bond through a surety company holding such grant of authority.

(b) Any person who willfully violates this section shall be fined not more than $10,000 or imprisoned for not more than one year, or both.

## Making of Loans; Payment of Fines

**Sec. 503.** (a) No labor organization shall make directly or indirectly any loan or loans to any officer or employee of such organization which results in a total indebtedness on the part of such officer or employee to the labor organization in excess of $2,000.

(b) No labor organization or employer shall directly or indirectly pay the fine of any officer or employee convicted of any willful violation of this Act.

(c) Any person who willfully violates this section shall be fined not more than $5,000 or imprisoned for not more than one year, or both.

## Prohibition Against Certain Persons Holding Office

**Sec. 504.** (a) No person who is or has been a member of the Communist Party or who has been convicted of, or served any part of a prison term resulting from his conviction of, robbery, bribery, extortion, embezzlement, grand larceny, burglary, arson, violation of narcotics laws, murder, rape, assault with intent to kill, assault which inflicts grievous bodily injury, or a violation of title II or III of this Act, any felony involving abuse or misuse of such person's position or employment in a labor organization or employee benefit plan to seek or obtain an illegal gain at the expense of the members of the labor organization or the beneficiaries of the employee benefit plan, or conspiracy to commit any such crimes or attempt to commit any such crimes, or a crime in which any of the foregoing crimes is an element, shall serve or be permitted to serve—

(1) as a consultant or adviser to any labor organization,

(2) as an officer, director, trustee, member of any executive board or similar governing body, business agent, manager, organizer, employee, or representative in any capacity of any labor organization,

(3) as a labor relations consultant or adviser to a person engaged in an industry or activity affecting commerce, or as an officer, director, agent, or employee of any group or association of employers dealing with any labor organization, or in a position having specific collective bargaining authority or direct responsibility in the area of labor-management relations in any corporation or association engaged in an industry or activity affecting commerce, or

(4) in a position which entitles its occupant to a share of the proceeds of, or as an officer or executive or administrative employee of, any entity whose activities are in whole or substantial part devoted to providing goods or services to any labor organization, or

(5) in any capacity, other than in his capacity as a member of such labor organization, that involves decisionmaking authority concerning, or decisionmaking authority over, or custody of, or control of the moneys, funds, assets, or property of any labor organization,

during or for the period of thirteen years after such conviction or after the end of such imprisonment, whichever is later, unless the sentencing court on the motion of the person convicted sets a lesser period of at least three years after such conviction or after the end of such imprisonment, whichever is later, or unless prior to the end of such period, in the case of a person so convicted or imprisoned, (A) his citizenship rights, having been revoked as a result of such conviction, have been fully restored, or (B) the United States Parole Commission determines that such person's service in any capacity referred to in clauses (1) through (5) would not be contrary to the purposes of this Act. Prior to making any such determination the Commission shall hold an administrative hearing and shall give notice of such proceeding by certified mail to the Secretary of Labor and to State, county, and Federal prosecuting officials in the jurisdiction or jurisdictions in which such person was convicted. The Commission's determination in any such proceeding shall be final. No person shall knowingly hire, retain, employ, or otherwise place any other person to serve in any capacity in violation of this subsection.

(b) Any person who willfully violates this section shall be fined not more than $10,000 or imprisoned for not more than five years, or both.

(c) For the purpose of this section—

(1) A person shall be deemed to have been 'convicted' and under the disability of 'conviction' from the date of the judgment of the trial court, regardless of whether that judgment remains under appeal.

(2) A period of parole shall not be considered as part of a period of imprisonment.

(d) Whenever any person—

(1) by operation of this section, has been barred from office or other position in a labor organization as a result of a conviction, and

(2) has filed an appeal of that conviction,

any salary which would be otherwise due such person by virtue of such office or position, shall be placed in escrow by the individual employer or organization responsible for payment of such salary. Payment of such salary into escrow shall continue for the duration of the appeal or for the period of time during which such salary would be otherwise due, whichever period is shorter. Upon the final reversal of such person's conviction on appeal, the amounts in escrow shall be paid to such person. Upon the final sustaining of such person's conviction on appeal, the amounts in escrow shall be returned to the individual employer or organization responsible for payments of those amounts. Upon final reversal of such person's conviction, such person shall no longer be barred by this statute from assuming any position from which such person was previously barred.*

## TITLE VI—MISCELLANEOUS PROVISIONS

### INVESTIGATIONS

**Sec. 601.** (a) The Secretary shall have power when he believes it necessary in order to determine whether any person has violated or is about to violate any provision of this Act (except title I or amendments made by this Act to other statutes) to make an investigation and in connection therewith he may enter such places and inspect such records and accounts and question such persons as he may deem necessary to enable him to determine the facts relative thereto. The Secretary may report to interested persons or officials concerning the facts required to be shown in any report required by this Act and concerning the reasons for failure or refusal to file such a report or any other matter which he deems to be appropriate as a result of such an investigation.

(b) For the purpose of any investigation provided for in this Act, the provisions of sections 9 and 10 (relating to the attendance of witnesses and the production of books, papers, and documents) of the Federal Trade Commission Act of September 16, 1914, as amended (15 U.S.C. 49, 50), are hereby made applicable to the jurisdiction, powers, and duties of the Secretary or any officers designated by him.

### EXTORTIONATE PICKETING

**Sec. 602.** (a) It shall be unlawful to carry on picketing on or about the premises of any employer for the purpose of, or as part of any conspiracy or in furtherance of any plan or purpose for, the personal profit or enrichment of any individual (except a bona fide increase in wages or other employee benefits) by taking or obtaining any money or other thing of value from such employer against his will or with his consent.

(b) Any person who willfully violates this section shall be fined not more than $10,000 or imprisoned not more than twenty years, or both.

---

* Section 504 was amended by Pub.L.No. 98–473, § 803, 98 Stat. 2133 (1984). Pub.L.No. 98–473, §§ 229, 235, 98 Stat. 2031 (1984), provided that, effective Nov. 1, 1986, subsec. (a) of this section is amended—

(a) by deleting "the Board of Parole of the United States Department of Justice" and substituting "if the offense is a Federal offense, the sentencing judge or, if the offense is a State or local offense, on motion of the United States Department of Justice, the district court of the United States for the district in which the offense was committed, pursuant to sentencing guidelines and policy statements issued pursuant to section 994(a) of Title 28,";

(b) by deleting "Board" and "Board's" and substituting "court" and "court's", respectively; and

(c) by deleting "an administrative" and substituting "a".

## RETENTION OF RIGHTS UNDER OTHER FEDERAL AND STATE LAWS

**Sec. 603.** (a) Except as explicitly provided to the contrary, nothing in this Act shall reduce or limit the responsibilities of any labor organization or any officer, agent, shop steward, or other representative of a labor organization, or of any trust in which a labor organization is interested, under any other Federal law or under the laws of any State, and, except as explicitly provided to the contrary, nothing in this Act shall take away any right or bar any remedy to which members of a labor organization are entitled under such other Federal law or law of any State.

(b) Nothing contained in titles I, II, III, IV, V, or VI of this Act shall be construed to supersede or impair or otherwise affect the provisions of the Railway Labor Act, as amended, or any of the obligations, rights, benefits, privileges, or immunities of any carrier, employee, organization, representative, or person subject thereto; nor shall anything contained in said titles (except section 505) of this Act be construed to confer any rights, privileges, immunities, or defenses upon employers, or to impair or otherwise affect the rights of any person under the National Labor Relations Act, as amended.

## EFFECT ON STATE LAWS

**Sec. 604.** Nothing in this Act shall be construed to impair or diminish the authority of any State to enact and enforce general criminal laws with respect to robbery, bribery, extortion, embezzlement, grand larceny, burglary, arson, violation of narcotics laws, murder, rape, assault with intent to kill, or assault which inflicts grievous bodily injury, or conspiracy to commit any of such crimes.

## SERVICE OF PROCESS

**Sec. 605.** For the purposes of this Act, service of summons, subpena, or other legal process of a court of the United States upon an officer or agent of a labor organization in his capacity as such shall constitute service upon the labor organization.

## ADMINISTRATIVE PROCEDURE ACT

**Sec. 606.** The provisions of the Administrative Procedure Act shall be applicable to the issuance, amendment, or rescission of any rules or regulations, or any adjudication, authorized or required pursuant to the provisions of this Act.

## OTHER AGENCIES AND DEPARTMENTS

**Sec. 607.** In order to avoid unnecessary expense and duplication of functions among Government agencies, the Secretary may make such arrangements or agreements for cooperation or mutual assistance in the performance of his functions under this Act and the functions of any such agency as he may find to be practicable and consistent with law. The Secretary may utilize the facilities or services of any department, agency, or establishment of the United States or of any State or political subdivision of a State, including the services of any of its employees, with the lawful consent of such department, agency, or establishment; and each department, agency, or establishment of the United States is authorized and directed to cooperate with the Secretary and, to the extent permitted by law, to provide such information and facilities as he may request for his assistance in the performance of his functions under this Act. The Attorney General or his representative shall receive from the Secretary for appropriate action such evidence developed in the performance of his functions under this Act as may be found to warrant consideration for criminal prosecution under the provisions of this Act or other Federal law.

## CRIMINAL CONTEMPT

**Sec. 608.** No person shall be punished for any criminal contempt allegedly committed outside the immediate presence of the court in connection with any civil action prosecuted by the Secretary or any other person in any court of the United States under the provisions of this Act unless the facts constituting such criminal contempt are established by the verdict of the jury in a proceeding in the district court of the United States, which jury shall be chosen and empaneled in the manner prescribed by the law governing trial juries in criminal prosecutions in the district courts of the United States.

## PROHIBITION ON CERTAIN DISCIPLINE BY LABOR ORGANIZATION

**Sec. 609.** It shall be unlawful for any labor organization, or any officer, agent, shop steward, or other representative of a labor organization, or any employee thereof to fine, suspend, expel, or otherwise discipline any of its members for exercising any right to which he is entitled under the provisions of this Act. The provisions of section 102 shall be applicable in the enforcement of this section.

## DEPRIVATION OF RIGHTS UNDER ACT BY VIOLENCE

**Sec. 610.** It shall be unlawful for any person through the use of force or violence, or threat of the use of force or violence, to restrain, coerce, or intimidate, or attempt to restrain, coerce, or intimidate any member of a labor organization for the purpose of interfering with or preventing the exercise of any right to which he is entitled under the provisions of this Act. Any person who willfully violates this section shall be fined not more than $1,000 or imprisoned for not more than one year, or both.

## Separability Provisions

**Sec. 611.** If any provision of this Act, or the application of such provision to any person or circumstances, shall be held invalid, the remainder of this Act or the application of such provision to persons or circumstances other than those as to which it is held invalid, shall not be affected thereby.

# TITLE VII, CIVIL RIGHTS ACT OF 1964

as amended by
Equal Employment Opportunity Act of 1972
78 Stat. 253 (1964), as amended by Pub.L. No. 92–261, March 24, 1972;
42 U.S.C. §§ 2000e et seq. (1982).

[*Note*: In setting forth the provisions of Title VII, no effort has been made to reflect the additions to and deletions from the 1964 Act effected by the 1972 Amendments. Title VII is simply set forth in its entirety, as amended. The 1972 changes are, however, outlined and discussed in the "Legislative Note" which appears, infra, immediately following the text of the statute. One aspect of the changes should, nonetheless, be brought to the reader's attention at the outset, to avoid confusion: Certain of the provisions of the 1964 Act have been renumbered in the amended statute. The old and new designations are listed below:

| OLD | NEW |
|---|---|
| § 705(b) | § 705(c) |
| 705(c) | 705(d) |
| 705(d) | 705(e) |
| 705(i) | 705(h) |
| 705(j) | 705(i) |
| 706(a) | 706(b) |
| 706(b) | 706(c) |
| 706(c) | 706(d) |
| 706(d) | 706(e) |
| 706(e) | 706(f) (1) |
| 706(f) | 706(f) (3). |

The following *totally* new sections were added:

§ 701(j)
705(b)
706(a)
706(f) (2), (4), (5)
707(c), (d), (e)
715
717
718.]

## DEFINITIONS

**Sec. 701.**   For the purposes of this title—

(a)  The term "person" includes one or more individuals, governments, governmental agencies, political subdivisions, labor unions, partnerships, associations, corporations, legal representatives, mutual companies, joint-stock companies, trusts, unincorporated organizations, trustees, trustees in cases under title 11, United States Code, or receivers.

(b) The term "employer" means a person engaged in an industry affecting commerce who has fifteen or more employees for each working day in each of twenty or more calendar weeks in the current or preceding calendar year, and any agent of such a person, but such term does not include (1) the United States, a corporation wholly owned ·by the Government of the United States, an Indian tribe, or any department or agency of the District of Columbia subject by statute to procedures of the competitive service (as defined in section 2102 of title 5 of the United States Code), or (2) a bona fide private membership club (other than a labor organization) which is exempt from taxation under section 501(c) of the Internal Revenue Code of 1954, except that during the first year after the date of enactment of the Equal Employment Opportunity Act of 1972, persons having fewer than twenty-five employees (and their agents) shall not be considered employers.

(c) The term "employment agency" means any person regularly undertaking with or without compensation to procure employees for an employer or to procure for employees opportunities to work for an employer and includes an agent of such a person.

(d) The term "labor organization" means a labor organization engaged in an industry affecting commerce, and any agent of such an organization, and includes any organization of any kind, any agency, or employee representation committee, group, association, or plan so engaged in which employees participate and which exists for the purpose, in whole or in part, of dealing with employers concerning grievances, labor disputes, wages, rates of pay, hours, or other terms or conditions of employment, and any conference, general committee, joint or system board, or joint council so engaged which is subordinate to a national or international labor organization.

(e) A labor organization shall be deemed to be engaged in an industry affecting commerce if (1) it maintains or operates a hiring hall or hiring office which procures employees for an employer or procures for employees opportunities to work for an employer, or (2) the number of its members (or, where it is a labor organization composed of other labor organizations or their representatives, if the aggregate number of the members of such other labor organization) is (A) twenty-five or more during the first year after the date of enactment of the Equal Employment Opportunity Act of 1972, or (B) fifteen or more thereafter, and such labor organization—

(1) is the certified representative of employees under the provisions of the National Labor Relations Act, as amended, or the Railway Labor Act, as amended;

(2) although not certified, is a national or international labor organization or a local labor organization recognized or acting as the representative of employees of an employer or employers engaged in an industry affecting commerce; or

(3) has chartered a local labor organization or subsidiary body which is representing or actively seeking to represent employees of employers within the meaning of paragraph (1) or (2); or

(4) has been chartered by a labor organization representing or actively seeking to represent employees within the meaning of paragraph (1) or (2) as the local or subordinate body through which such employees may enjoy membership or become affiliated with such labor organization; or

(5) is a conference, general committee, joint or system board, or joint council subordinate to a national or international labor organization, which includes a labor organization engaged in an industry affecting commerce within the meaning of any of the preceding paragraphs of this subsection.

(f) The term "employee" means an individual employed by an employer, except that the term "employee" shall not include any person elected to public office in any State or political subdivision of any State by the qualified voters thereof, or any person chosen by such officer to be on such officer's personal staff, or an appointee on the policy making level or an immediate adviser with respect to the exercise of the constitutional or legal powers of the office. The exemption set forth in the preceding sentence shall not include employees subject to the civil service laws of a State government, governmental agency or political subdivision.

(g) The term "commerce" means trade, traffic, commerce, transportation, transmission, or communication among the several States; or between a State and any place outside thereof; or within the District of Columbia, or a possession of the United States; or between points in the same State but through a point outside thereof.

(h) The term "industry affecting commerce" means any activity, business, or industry in commerce or in which a labor dispute would hinder or obstruct commerce or the free flow of commerce and includes any activity or industry "affecting commerce" within the meaning of the Labor-Management Reporting and Disclosure Act of 1959, and further includes any governmental industry, business, or activity.

(i) The term "State" includes a State of the United States, the District of Columbia, Puerto Rico, the Virgin Islands, American Samoa, Guam, Wake Island, the Canal Zone, and Outer Continental Shelf lands defined in the Outer Continental Shelf Lands Act.

(j) The term "religion" includes all aspects of religious observance and practice, as well as belief, unless an employer demonstrates that he is unable to reasonably accommodate to an employee's or prospective employee's religious observance or practice without undue hardship on the conduct of the employer's business.

(k) The terms 'because of sex' or 'on the basis of sex' include, but are not limited to, because of or on the basis of pregnancy, childbirth, or related medical conditions; and women affected by pregnancy, childbirth, or related medical conditions shall be treated the same for all employment-related purposes, including receipt of benefits under fringe benefit programs, as other persons not so affected but similar in their ability or inability to work, and nothing in section 703 (h) of this title shall be interpreted to permit otherwise. This subsection shall not require an employer to pay for health insurance benefits for abortion, except where the life of the mother would be endangered if the fetus were carried to term, or except where medical complications have arisen from an abortion: *Provided,* That nothing herein shall preclude an employer from providing abortion benefits or otherwise affect bargaining agreements in regard to abortion.*

EXEMPTION

**Sec. 702.** This title shall not apply to an employer with respect to the employment of aliens outside any State, or to a religious corporation, association, educational institution, or society with respect to the employment of individuals of a particular religion to perform work connected with the carrying on by such corporation, association, educational institution, or society of its activities.

DISCRIMINATION BECAUSE OF RACE, COLOR, RELIGION, SEX, OR NATIONAL ORIGIN

**Sec. 703.** (a) It shall be an unlawful employment practice for an employer—

(1) to fail or refuse to hire or to discharge any individual or otherwise to discriminate against any individual with respect to his compensation, terms, conditions, or privileges of employment, because of such individual's race, color, religion, sex, or national origin; or

(2) to limit, segregate, or classify his employees or applicants for employment in any way which would deprive or tend to deprive any individual of employment opportunities or otherwise adversely affect his status as an employee, because of such individual's race, color, religion, sex, or national origin.

* Subsection (k) was enacted by Pub.L.No. 95–555, § 1, 92 Stat. 2076 (1978).

(b) It shall be an unlawful employment practice for an employment agency to fail or refuse to refer for employment, or otherwise to discriminate against, any individual because of his race, color, religion, sex, or national origin, or to classify or refer for employment any individual on the basis of his race, color, religion, sex or national origin.

(c) It shall be an unlawful employment practice for a labor organization—

(1) to exclude or to expel from its membership, or otherwise to discriminate against, any individual because of his race, color, religion, sex, or national origin;

(2) to limit, segregate, or classify its membership or applicants for membership, or to classify or fail or refuse to refer for employment any individual, in any way which would deprive or tend to deprive any individual of employment opportunities, or would limit such employment opportunities or otherwise adversely affect his status as an employee or as an applicant for employment, because of such individual's race, color, religion, sex, or national origin; or

(3) to cause or attempt to cause an employer to discriminate against an individual in violation of this section.

(d) It shall be an unlawful employment practice for any employer, labor organization, or joint labor-management committee controlling apprenticeship or other training or retraining, including on-the-job training programs to discriminate against any individual because of his race, color, religion, sex, or national origin in admission to, or employment in, any program established to provide apprenticeship or other training.

(e) Notwithstanding any other provision of this title, (1) it shall not be an unlawful employment practice for an employer to hire and employ employees, for an employment agency to classify, or refer for employment any individual, for a labor organization to classify its membership or to classify or refer for employment any individual, or for an employer, labor organization, or joint labor-management committee controlling apprenticeship or other training or retraining programs to admit or employ any individual in any such program, on the basis of his religion, sex, or national origin in those certain instances where religion, sex, or national origin is a bona fide occupational qualification reasonably necessary to the normal operation of that particular business or enterprise, and (2) it shall not be an unlawful employment practice for a school, college, university, or other educational institution or institution of learning to hire and employ employees of a particular religion if such school, college, university, or other educational institution or institution of learning is, in whole or in substantial part, owned, supported, controlled, or managed by a particular religion or by a particular religious corporation, association, or society, or if the curriculum of such school, college, university, or other educational institution or institution of learning is directed toward the propagation of a particular religion.

(f) As used in this title, the phrase "unlawful employment practice" shall not be deemed to include any action or measure taken by an employer, labor organization, joint labor-management committee, or employment agency with respect to an individual who is a member of the Communist Party of the United States or of any other organization required to register as a Communist-action or Communist-front organization by final order of the Subversive Activities Control Board pursuant to the Subversive Activities Control Act of 1950.

(g) Notwithstanding any other provision of this title, it shall not be an unlawful employment practice for an employer to fail or refuse to hire and employ any individual for any position, for an employer to discharge any individual from any position, or for an employment agency to fail or refuse to refer any individual for employment in any position, or for a labor organization to fail or refuse to refer any individual for employment in any position, if—

(1) the occupancy of such position, or access to the premises in or upon which any part of the duties of such position is performed or is to be performed, is subject to any requirement imposed in the interest of the national security of the United States under any security program in effect pursuant to or administered under any statute of the United States or any Executive order of the President; and

(2) such individual has not fulfilled or has ceased to fulfill that requirement.

(h) Notwithstanding any other provision of this title, it shall not be an unlawful employment practice for an employer to apply different standards of compensation, or different terms, conditions, or privileges of employment pursuant to a bona fide seniority or merit system, or a system which measures earnings by quantity or quality of production or to employees who work in different locations, provided that such differences are not the result of an intention to discriminate because of race, color, religion, sex, or national origin; nor shall it be an unlawful employment practice for an employer to give and to act upon the results of any professionally developed ability test provided that such test, its administration or action upon the results is not designed, intended, or used to discriminate because of race, color, religion, sex, or national origin. It shall not be an unlawful employment practice under this title for any employer to differentiate upon the basis of sex in determining the amount of the wages or compensation paid or to be paid to employees of such employer if such differentiation is authorized by the provisions of Section 6(d) of the Fair Labor Standards Act of 1938, as amended (29 U.S.C. 206(d) ).

(i) Nothing contained in this title shall apply to any business or enterprise on or near an Indian reservation with respect to any publicly announced employment practice of such business or enterprise under which a preferential treatment is given to any individual because he is an Indian living on or near a reservation.

(j) Nothing contained in this title shall be interpreted to require any employer, employment agency, labor organization, or joint labor-management committee subject to this title to grant preferential treatment to any individual or to any group because of the race, color, religion, sex, or national origin of such individual or group on account of an imbalance which may exist with respect to the total number or percentage of persons of any race, color, religion, sex, or national origin employed by any employer, referred or classified for employment by any employment agency or labor organization, admitted to membership or classified by any labor organization, or admitted to, or employed in, any apprenticeship or other training program, in comparison with the total number or percentage of persons of such race, color, religion, sex, or national origin in any community, State, section, or other area, or in the available work force in any community, State, section, or other area.

## OTHER UNLAWFUL EMPLOYMENT PRACTICES

**Sec. 704.** (a) It shall be an unlawful employment practice for an employer to discriminate against any of his employees or applicants for employment, for an employment agency, or joint labor-management committee controlling apprenticeship or other training or retraining, including on-the-job training programs, to discriminate against any individual, or for a labor organization to discriminate against any member thereof or applicant for membership, because he has opposed any practice made an unlawful employment practice by this title, or because he has made a charge, testified, assisted, or participated in any manner in an investigation, proceeding, or hearing under this title.

(b) It shall be an unlawful employment practice for an employer, labor organization, employment agency, or joint labor-management committee controlling apprenticeship or other training or retraining, including on-the-job training programs, to print or publish or cause to be printed or published any notice or advertisement relating to employment by such an employer or membership in or any classification or referral for employment by such a labor organization, or relating to any classification or referral for employment by such an employment agency, or relating to admission to, or employment in, any program established to provide apprenticeship or other training by such a joint labor-management committee indicating any preference, limitation, specification, or discrimination, based on race, color, religion, sex, or national origin, except that such a notice or advertisement may indicate a preference, limitation, specification, or discrimination based on religion, sex, or national origin when religion, sex, or national origin is a bona fide occupational qualification for employment.

## EQUAL EMPLOYMENT OPPORTUNITY COMMISSION

**Sec. 705.** (a) There is hereby created a Commission to be known as the Equal Employment Opportunity Commission, which shall be composed of five members, not more than three of whom shall be members of the same political party. Members of the Commission shall be appointed by the President by and with the advice and consent of the Senate for a term of five years. Any individual chosen to fill a vacancy shall be appointed only for the unexpired term of the member whom he shall succeed, and all members of the Commission shall continue to serve until their successors are appointed and qualified, except that no such member of the Commission shall continue to serve (1) for more than sixty days when the Congress is in session unless a nomination to fill such vacancy shall have been submitted to the Senate, or (2) after the adjournment sine die of the session of the Senate in which such nomination was submitted. The President shall designate one member to serve as Chairman of the Commission, and one member to serve as Vice Chairman. The Chairman shall be responsible on behalf of the Commission for the administrative operations of the Commission, and, except as provided in subsection (b), shall appoint, in accordance with the provisions of title 5, United States Code, governing appointments in the competitive service, such officers, agents, attorneys, administrative law judges, and employees as he deems necessary to assist it in the performance of its functions and to fix their compensation in accordance with the provisions of chapter 51 and subchapter III of chapter 53 of title 5, United States Code, relating to classification and General Schedule pay rates: *Provided,* That assignment, removal, and compensation of administrative law judges shall be in accordance with sections 3105, 3344, 5362,* and 7521 of title 5, United States Code.

(b) (1) There shall be a General Counsel of the Commission appointed by the President, by and with the advice and consent of the Senate, for a term of four years. The General Counsel shall have responsibility for the conduct of litigation as provided in sections 706 and 707 of this title. The General Counsel shall have such other duties as the Commission may prescribe or as may be provided by law and shall concur with the Chairman of the Commission on the appointment and supervision of regional attorneys. The General Counsel of the Commission on the effective date of this Act shall continue in such position and perform the functions specified in this subsection until a successor is appointed and qualified.

(2) Attorneys appointed under this section may, at the direction of the Commission, appear for and represent the Commission in any case in court, provided that the Attorney General shall conduct all litigation to which the Commission is a party in the Supreme Court pursuant to this title.

---

* 5 U.S.C. § 5362 was redesignated as 5 U.S.C. § 5372 by Pub. L. No. 95–454, § 801(a)(3)(A)(ii), 92 Stat. 1221 (1978).

(c) A vacancy in the Commission shall not impair the right of the remaining members to exercise all the powers of the Commission and three members thereof shall constitute a quorum.

(d) The Commission shall have an official seal which shall be judicially noticed.

(e) The Commission shall at the close of each fiscal year report to the Congress and to the President concerning the action it has taken and the moneys it has disbursed. It shall make such further reports on the cause of and means of eliminating discrimination and such recommendations for further legislation as may appear desirable.

(f) The principal office of the Commission shall be in or near the District of Columbia, but it may meet or exercise any or all its powers at any other place. The Commission may establish such regional or State offices as it deems necessary to accomplish the purpose of this title.

(g) The Commission shall have power—

(1) to cooperate with and, with their consent, utilize regional, State, local, and other agencies, both public and private, and individuals;

(2) to pay to witnesses whose depositions are taken or who are summoned before the Commission or any of its agents the same witness and mileage fees as are paid to witnesses in the courts of the United States;

(3) to furnish to persons subject to this title such technical assistance as they may request to further their compliance with this title or an order issued thereunder;

(4) upon the request of (i) any employer, whose employees or some of them, or (ii) any labor organization, whose members or some of them, refuse or threaten to refuse to cooperate in effectuating the provisions of this title, to assist in such effectuation by conciliation or such other remedial action as is provided by this title;

(5) to make such technical studies as are appropriate to effectuate the purposes and policies of this title and to make the results of such studies available to the public;

(6) to intervene in a civil action brought under section 706 by an aggrieved party against a respondent other than a government, governmental agency or political subdivision.

(h) The Commission shall, in any of its educational or promotional activities, cooperate with other departments and agencies in the performance of such educational and promotional activities.

(i) All officers, agents, attorneys and employees of the Commission, including the members of the Commission, shall be subject to the provisions of section 9 of the act of August 2, 1939, as amended (Hatch Act), notwithstanding any exemption contained in such section.

## PREVENTION OF UNLAWFUL EMPLOYMENT PRACTICES

**Sec. 706.** (a) The Commission is empowered, as hereinafter provided, to prevent any person from engaging in any unlawful employment practice as set forth in section 703 or 704 of this title.

(b) Whenever a charge is filed by or on behalf of a person claiming to be aggrieved, or by a member of the Commission, alleging that an employer, employment agency, labor organization, or joint labor-management committee controlling apprenticeship or other training or retraining, including on-the-job training programs, has engaged in an unlawful employment practice, the Commission shall serve a notice of the charge (including the date, place and circumstances of the alleged unlawful employment practice) on such employer, employment agency, labor organization, or joint labor-management committee (hereinafter referred to as the "respondent") within ten days, and shall make an investigation thereof. Charges shall be in writing under oath or affirmation and shall contain such information and be in such form as the Commission requires. Charges shall not be made public by the Commission. If the Commission determines after such investigation that there is not reasonable cause to believe that the charge is true, it shall dismiss the charge and promptly notify the person claiming to be aggrieved and the respondent of its action. In determining whether reasonable cause exists, the Commission shall accord substantial weight to final findings and orders made by State or local authorities in proceedings commenced under State or local law pursuant to the requirements of subsections (c) and (d). If the Commission determines after such investigation that there is reasonable cause to believe that the charge is true, the Commission shall endeavor to eliminate any such alleged unlawful employment practice by informal methods of conference, conciliation, and persuasion. Nothing said or done during and as a part of such informal endeavors may be made public by the Commission, its officers or employees, or used as evidence in a subsequent proceeding without the written consent of the persons concerned. Any person who makes public information in violation of this subsection shall be fined not more than $1,000 or imprisoned for not more than one year, or both. The Commission shall make its determination on reasonable cause as promptly as possible and, so far as practicable, not later than one hundred and twenty days from the filing of the charge or, where applicable under subsection (c) or (d), from the date upon which the Commission is authorized to take action with respect to the charge.

(c) In the case of an alleged unlawful employment practice occurring in a State, or political subdivision of a State, which has a State or local law prohibiting the unlawful employment practice alleged and establishing or authorizing a State or local authority to grant or seek relief from such practice or to institute criminal proceedings with respect thereto upon receiving notice thereof, no charge may be filed under subsection (b) by the person aggrieved before the expiration of sixty days after proceedings have been commenced under the State or local law, unless such proceedings have been earlier terminated, provided that such sixty-day period shall be extended to one hundred and twenty days during the first year after the effective date of such State or local law. If any requirement for the commencement of such proceedings is imposed by a State or local authority other than a requirement of the filing of a written and signed statement of the facts upon which the proceeding is based, the proceeding shall be deemed to have been commenced for the purposes of this subsection at the time such statement is sent by registered mail to the appropriate State or local authority.

(d) In the case of any charge filed by a member of the Commission alleging an unlawful employment practice occurring in a State or political subdivision of a State which has a State or local law prohibiting the practice alleged and establishing or authorizing a State or local authority to grant or seek relief from such practice or to institute criminal proceedings with respect thereto upon receiving notice thereof, the Commission shall, before taking any action with respect to such charge, notify the appropriate State or local officials and, upon request, afford them a reasonable time, but not less than sixty days (provided that such sixty-day period shall be extended to one hundred and twenty days during the first year after the effective day of such State or local law), unless a shorter period is requested, to act under such State or local law to remedy the practice alleged.

(e) A charge under this section shall be filed within one hundred and eighty days after the alleged unlawful employment practice occurred and notice of the charge (including the date, place and circumstances of the alleged unlawful employment practice) shall be served upon the person against whom such charge is made within ten days thereafter, except that in a case of an unlawful employment practice with respect to which the person aggrieved has initially instituted proceedings with a State or local agency with authority to grant or seek relief from such practice or to institute criminal proceedings with respect thereto upon receiving notice thereof, such charge shall be filed by or on behalf of the person aggrieved within three hundred days after the alleged unlawful employment practice occurred, or within thirty days after receiving notice that the State or local agency has terminated the proceedings under the State or local law, whichever is earlier, and a copy of such charge shall be filed by the Commission with the State or local agency.

(f) (1) If within thirty days after a charge is filed with the Commission or within thirty days after expiration of any period of reference under subsection (c) or (d), the Commission has been unable to secure from the respondent a conciliation agreement acceptable to the Commission, the Commission may bring a civil action against any respondent not a government, governmental agency, or political subdivision named in the charge. In the case of a respondent which is a government, governmental agency, or political subdivision, if the Commission has been unable to secure from the respondent a conciliation agreement acceptable to the Commission, the Commission shall take no further action and shall refer the case to the Attorney General who may bring a civil action against such respondent in the appropriate United States district court. The person or persons aggrieved shall have the right to intervene in a civil action brought by the Commission or the Attorney General in a case involving a government, governmental agency, or political subdivision. If a charge filed with the Commission pursuant to subsection (b) is dismissed by the Commission, or if within one hundred and eighty days from the filing of such charge or the expiration of any period of reference under subsection (c) or (d), whichever is later, the Commission has not filed a civil action under this section or the Attorney General has not filed a civil action in a case involving a government, governmental agency, or political subdivision, or the Commission has not entered into a conciliation agreement to which the person aggrieved is a party, the Commission, or the Attorney General in a case involving a government, governmental agency, or political subdivision, shall so notify the person aggrieved and within ninety days after the giving of such notice a civil action may be brought against the respondent named in the charge (A) by the person claiming to be aggrieved or (B) if such charge was filed by a member of the Commission, by any person whom the charge alleges was aggrieved by the alleged unlawful employment practice. Upon application by the complainant and in such circumstances as the court may deem just, the court may appoint an attorney for such complainant and may authorize the commencement of the action without the payment of fees, costs, or security. Upon timely application, the court may, in its discretion, permit the Commission, or the Attorney General in a case involving a government, governmental agency, or political subdivision, to intervene in such civil action upon certification that the case is of general public importance. Upon request, the court may, in its discretion, stay further proceedings for not more than sixty days pending the termination of State or local proceedings described in subsections (c) or (d) of this section or further efforts of the Commission to obtain voluntary compliance.

(2) Whenever a charge is filed with the Commission and the Commission concludes on the basis of a preliminary investigation that prompt judicial action is necessary to carry out the purposes of this Act, the Commission, or the Attorney General in a case involving a government, governmental agency, or political subdivision, may bring an action for appropriate temporary or preliminary relief pending final disposition of such charge. Any temporary restraining order or other order granting preliminary or temporary relief shall be issued in accordance with rule 65 of the Federal Rules of Civil Procedure. It shall be the duty of a court having jurisdiction over proceedings under this section to assign cases for hearing at the earliest practicable date and to cause such cases to be in every way expedited.

(3) Each United States district court and each United States court of a place subject to the jurisdiction of the United States shall

have jurisdiction of actions brought under this title. Such an action may be brought in any judicial district in the State in which the unlawful employment practice is alleged to have been committed, in the judicial district in which the employment records relevant to such practice are maintained and administered, or in the judicial district in which the aggrieved person would have worked but for the alleged unlawful employment practice, but if the respondent is not found within any such district, such an action may be brought within the judicial district in which the respondent has his principal office. For purposes of sections 1404 and 1406 of title 28 of the United States Code, the judicial district in which the respondent has his principal office shall in all cases be considered a district in which the action might have been brought.

(4) It shall be the duty of the chief judge of the district (or in his absence, the acting chief judge) in which the case is pending immediately to designate a judge in such district to hear and determine the case. In the event that no judge in the district is available to hear and determine the case, the chief judge of the district, or the acting chief judge, as the case may be, shall certify this fact to the chief judge of the circuit (or in his absence, the acting chief judge) who shall then designate a district or circuit judge of the circuit to hear and determine the case.

(5) It shall be the duty of the judge designated pursuant to this subsection to assign the case for hearing at the earliest practicable date and to cause the case to be in every way expedited. If such judge has not scheduled the case for trial within one hundred and twenty days after issue has been joined, that judge may appoint a master pursuant to rule 53 of the Federal Rules of Civil Procedure.

(g) If the court finds that the respondent has intentionally engaged in or is intentionally engaging in an unlawful employment practice charged in the complaint, the court may enjoin the respondent from engaging in such unlawful employment practice, and order such affirmative action as may be appropriate, which may include, but is not limited to, reinstatement or hiring of employees, with or without back pay (payable by the employer, employment agency, or labor organization, as the case may be, responsible for the unlawful employment practice), or any other equitable relief as the court deems appropriate. Back pay liability shall not accrue from a date more than two years prior to the filing of a charge with the Commission. Interim earnings or amounts earnable with reasonable diligence by the person or persons discriminated against shall operate to reduce the back pay otherwise allowable. No order of the court shall require the admission or reinstatement of an individual as a member of a union, or the hiring, reinstatement, or promotion of an individual as an employee, or the payment to him of any back pay, if such individual was refused admission, suspended, or expelled, or was refused employment or advancement or was suspended or discharged for any reason other than discrimination on account of race, color, religion, sex, or national origin or in violation of section 704(a).

(h) The provisions of the Act entitled "An Act to amend the Judicial Code and to define and limit the jurisdiction of courts sitting in equity, and for other purposes," approved March 23, 1932 (29 U.S.C. 101–115), shall not apply with respect to civil actions brought under this section.

(i) In any case in which an employer, employment agency, or labor organization fails to comply with an order of a court issued in a civil action brought under this section the Commission may commence proceedings to compel compliance with such order.

(j) Any civil action brought under this section and any proceedings brought under subsection (i) shall be subject to appeal as provided in sections 1291 and 1292, title 28, United States Code.

(k) In any action or proceeding under this title the court, in its discretion, may allow the prevailing party, other than the Commission or the United States, a reasonable attorney's fee as part of the costs, and the Commission and the United States shall be liable for costs the same as a private person.

Sec. 707.  (a) Whenever the Attorney General has reasonable cause to believe that any person or group of persons is engaged in a pattern or practice of resistance to the full enjoyment of any of the rights secured by this title, and that the pattern or practice is of such a nature and is intended to deny the full exercise of the rights herein described, the Attorney General may bring a civil action in the appropriate district court of the United States by filing with it a complaint (1) signed by him (or in his absence the Acting Attorney General), (2) setting forth facts pertaining to such pattern or practice, and (3) requesting such relief, including an application for a permanent or temporary injunction, restraining order or other order against the person or persons responsible for such pattern or practice, as he deems necessary to insure the full enjoyment of the rights herein described.

(b) The district courts of the United States shall have and shall exercise jurisdiction of proceedings instituted pursuant to this section, and in any such proceeding the Attorney General may file with the clerk of such court a request that a court of three judges be convened to hear and determine the case.  Such request by the Attorney General shall be accompanied by a certificate that, in his opinion, the case is of general public importance.  A copy of the certificate and request for a three-judge court shall be immediately furnished by such clerk to the chief judge of the circuit (or in his absence, the presiding circuit judge of the circuit) in which the case is pending.  Upon receipt of such request it shall be the duty of the chief judge of the circuit or the presiding circuit judge, as the case may be, to designate immediately three judges in such circuit, of whom at least one shall be a circuit judge and another of whom shall be a district judge of the court in which the proceeding was instituted, to hear and determine such case, and it shall be the duty of the judges so designated to assign the case for hearing at the earliest practicable date, to participate in the hearing and determination thereof, and to cause the case to be in every way expedited. An appeal from the final judgment of such court will lie to the Supreme Court.

In the event the Attorney General fails to file such a request in any such proceeding, it shall be the duty of the chief judge of the district (or in his absence, the acting chief judge) in which the case is pending immediately to designate a judge in such district to hear and determine the case. In the event that no judge in the district is available to hear and determine the case, the chief judge of the district, or the acting chief judge, as the case may be, shall certify this fact to the chief judge of the circuit (or in his absence, the acting chief judge) who shall then designate a district or circuit judge of the circuit to hear and determine the case.

It shall be the duty of the judge designated pursuant to this section to assign the case for hearing at the earliest practicable date and to cause the case to be in every way expedited.

(c) Effective two years after the date of enactment of the Equal Employment Opportunity Act of 1972, the functions of the Attorney General under this section shall be transferred to the Commission, together with such personnel, property, records, and unexpended balances of appropriations, allocations, and other funds employed, used, held, available, or to be made available in connection with such functions unless the President submits, and neither House of Congress vetoes, a reorganization plan pursuant to chapter 9 of title 5, United States Code, inconsistent with the provisions of this subsection. The Commission shall carry out such functions in accordance with subsections (d) and (e) of this section.

(d) Upon the transfer of functions provided for in subsection (c) of this section, in all suits commenced pursuant to this section prior to the date of such transfer, proceedings shall continue without abatement, all court orders and decrees shall remain in effect, and the Commission shall be substituted as a party for the United States of America, the Attorney General, or the Acting Attorney General, as appropriate.

(e) Subsequent to the date of enactment of the Equal Employment Opportunity Act of 1972, the Commission shall have authority to investigate and act on a charge of a pattern or practice of discrimination, whether filed by or on behalf of a person claiming to be aggrieved or by a member of the Commission. All such actions shall be conducted in accordance with the procedures set forth in section 706 of this Act.

### EFFECT ON STATE LAWS

**Sec. 708.** Nothing in this title shall be deemed to exempt or relieve any person from any liability, duty, penalty, or punishment provided by any present or future law of any State or political subdivision of a State, other than any such law which purports to require or permit the doing of any act which would be an unlawful employment practice under this title.

INVESTIGATIONS, INSPECTIONS, RECORDS, STATE AGENCIES

**Sec. 709.** (a) In connection with any investigation of a charge filed under section 706, the Commission or its designated representative shall at all reasonable times have access to, for the purposes of examination, and the right to copy any evidence of any person being investigated or proceeded against that relates to unlawful employment practices covered by this title and is relevant to the charge under investigation.

(b) The Commission may cooperate with State and local agencies charged with the administration of State fair employment practices laws and, with the consent of such agencies, may, for the purpose of carrying out its functions and duties under this title and within the limitation of funds appropriated specifically for such purpose, engage in and contribute to the cost of research and other projects of mutual interest undertaken by such agencies, and utilize the services of such agencies and their employees, and, notwithstanding any other provision of law, pay by advance or reimbursement such agencies and their employees for services rendered to assist the Commission in carrying out this title. In furtherance of such cooperative efforts, the Commission may enter into written agreements with such State or local agencies and such agreements may include provisions under which the Commission shall refrain from processing a charge in any cases or class of cases specified in such agreements or under which the Commission shall relieve any person or class of persons in such State or locality from requirements imposed under this section. The Commission shall rescind any such agreement whenever it determines that the agreement no longer serves the interest of effective enforcement of this title.

(c) Every employer, employment agency, and labor organization subject to this title shall (1) make and keep such records relevant to the determinations of whether unlawful employment practices have been or are being committed, (2) preserve such records for such periods, and (3) make such reports therefrom as the Commission shall prescribe by regulation or order, after public hearing, as reasonable, necessary, or appropriate for the enforcement of this title or the regulations or orders thereunder. The Commission shall, by regulation, require each employer, labor organization, and joint labor-management committee subject to this title which controls an apprenticeship or other training program to maintain such records as are reasonably necessary to carry out the purposes of this title, including, but not limited to, a list of applicants who wish to participate in such program, including the chronological order in which applications were received, and to furnish to the Commission upon request, a detailed description of the manner in which persons are selected to participate in the apprenticeship or other training program. Any employer, employment agency, labor organization, or joint labor-management committee which believes that the application to it of any regulation or order issued under this section would result in undue hardship may apply to the Commission for an exemption from the application of such regulation or order, and, if such application for an exemption is denied, bring a civil action in the United States district court for the district where such records are kept. If the Commission or the court, as the case may be, finds that the application of the regulation or order to the employer, employment agency, or labor organization in question would impose an undue hardship, the Commission or the court, as the case may be, may grant appropriate relief. If any person required to comply with the provisions of this subsection fails or refuses to do so, the United States district court for the district in which such person is found, resides, or transacts business, shall, upon application of the Commission, or the Attorney General in a case involving a government, governmental agency or political subdivision, have jurisdiction to issue to such person an order requiring him to comply.

(d) In prescribing requirements pursuant to subsection (c) of this section, the Commission shall consult with other interested State and Federal agencies and shall endeavor to coordinate its requirements with those adopted by such agencies. The Commission shall furnish upon request and without cost to any State or local agency charged with the administration of a fair employment practice law information obtained pursuant to subsection (c) of this section from any employer, employment agency, labor organization, or joint labor-management committee subject to the jurisdiction of such agency. Such information shall be furnished on condition that it not be made public by the recipient agency prior to the institution of a proceeding under State or local law involving such information. If this condition is violated by a recipient agency, the Commission may decline to honor subsequent requests pursuant to this subsection.

(e) It shall be unlawful for any officer or employee of the Commission to make public in any manner whatever any information obtained by the Commission pursuant to its authority under this section prior to the institution of any proceeding under this title involving such information. Any officer or employee of the Commission who shall make public in any manner whatever any information in violation of this subsection shall be guilty of a misdemeanor and upon conviction thereof, shall be fined not more than $1,000, or imprisoned not more than one year.

## INVESTIGATORY POWERS

**Sec. 710.** For the purpose of all hearings and investigations conducted by the Commission or its duly authorized agents or agencies, section 11 of the National Labor Relations Act (49 Stat. 455; 29 U.S.C. 161) shall apply.

## NOTICES TO BE POSTED

**Sec. 711.** (a) Every employer, employment agency, and labor organization, as the case may be, shall post and keep posted in conspicuous places upon its premises where notices to employees, applicants for employment, and members are customarily posted a notice to be prepared or approved by the Commission setting forth excerpts from, or summaries of, the pertinent provisions of this title and information pertinent to the filing of a complaint.

(b) A willful violation of this section shall be punishable by a fine of not more than $100 for each separate offense.

## VETERANS' PREFERENCE

**Sec. 712.** Nothing contained in this title shall be construed to repeal or modify any Federal, State, territorial, or local law creating special rights or preference for veterans.

## RULES AND REGULATIONS

**Sec. 713.** (a) The Commission shall have authority from time to time to issue, amend, or rescind suitable procedural regulations to carry out the provisions of this title. Regulations issued under this section shall be in conformity with the standards and limitations of the Administrative Procedure Act.

(b) In any action or proceeding based on any alleged unlawful employment practice, no person shall be subject to any liability or punishment for or on account of (1) the commission by such person of an unlawful employment practice if he pleads and proves that the act or omission complained of was in good faith, in conformity with, and in reliance on any written interpretation or opinion of the Commission, or (2) the failure of such person to publish and file any information required by any provision of this title if he pleads and proves that he failed to publish and file such information in good faith, in conformity with the instructions of the Commission issued under this title regarding the filing of such information. Such a defense, if established, shall be a bar to the action or proceeding, notwithstanding that (A) after such act or omission, such interpretation or opinion is modified or rescinded or is determined by judicial authority to be invalid or of no legal effect, or (B) after publishing or filing the description and annual reports, such publication or filing is determined by judicial authority not to be in conformity with the requirements of this title.

FORCIBLY RESISTING THE COMMISSION OR ITS
REPRESENTATIVES

**Sec. 714.**    The provisions of sections 111 and 1114, title 18, United States Code, shall apply to officers, agents, and employees of the Commission in the performance of their official duties.    Notwithstanding the provisions of sections 111 and 1114 of title 18, United States Code, whoever in violation of the provisions of section 1114 of such title kills a person while engaged in or on account of the performance of his official functions under this Act shall be punished by imprisonment for any term of years or for life.

EQUAL EMPLOYMENT OPPORTUNITY COORDINATING COUNCIL

**Sec. 715.**    There shall be established an Equal Employment Opportunity Coordinating Council (hereinafter referred to in this section as the Council) composed of the Secretary of Labor, the Chairman of the Equal Employment Opportunity Commission, the Attorney General, the Chairman of the United States Civil Service Commission, and the Chairman of the United States Civil Rights Commission, or their respective delegates.    The Council shall have the responsibility for developing and implementing agreements, policies and practices designed to maximize effort, promote efficiency, and eliminate conflict, competition, duplication and inconsistency among the operations, functions and jurisdictions of the various departments, agencies and branches of the Federal Government responsible for the implementation and enforcement of equal employment opportunity legislation, orders, and policies.    On or before October 1 of each year, the Council shall transmit to the President and to the Congress a report of its activities, together with such recommendations for legislative or administrative changes as it concludes are desirable to further promote the purposes of this section.*

EFFECTIVE DATE

**Sec. 716.**    (a) This title shall become effective one year after the date of its enactment.

(b) Notwithstanding subsection (a), sections of this title other than sections 703, 704, 706, and 707 shall become effective immediately.

(c) The President shall, as soon as feasible after the enactment of this title, convene one or more conferences for the purpose of enabling the leaders of groups whose members will be affected by this title to become familiar with the rights afforded and obligations imposed by its provisions, and for the purpose of making plans which will result in the fair and effective administration of this title when all

---

* The Equal Employment Opportunity Coordinating Council was abolished and its functions transferred to the Equal Employment Opportunity Commission by Reorg. Plan No. 1 of 1978, § 6, 3 C.F.R. 321 (1978), *reprinted in* 5 U.S.C. App. at 1155 (1982), *and in* 92 Stat. 3782 (1978).

of its provisions become effective. The President shall invite the participation in such conference or conferences of (1) the members of the President's Committee on Equal Employment Opportunity, (2) the members of the Commission on Civil Rights, (3) representatives of State and local agencies engaged in furthering equal employment opportunity, (4) representatives of private agencies engaged in furthering equal employment opportunity, and (5) representatives of employers, labor organizations, and employment agencies who will be subject to this title.

## NONDISCRIMINATION IN FEDERAL GOVERNMENT EMPLOYMENT

**Sec. 717.** (a) All personnel actions affecting employees or applicants for employment (except with regard to aliens employed outside the limits of the United States) in military departments as defined in section 102 of title 5, United States Code, in executive agencies as defined in section 105 of title 5, United States Code (including employees and applicants for employment who are paid from nonappropriated funds), in the United States Postal Service and the Postal Rate Commission, in those units of the Government of the District of Columbia having positions in the competitive service, and in those units of the legislative and judicial branches of the Federal Government having positions in the competitive service, and in the Library of Congress shall be made free from any discrimination based on race, color, religion, sex, or national origin.

(b) Except as otherwise provided in this subsection, the Civil Service Commission shall have authority to enforce the provisions of subsection (a) through appropriate remedies, including reinstatement or hiring of employees with or without back pay, as will effectuate the policies of this section, and shall issue such rules, regulations, orders and instructions as it deems necessary and appropriate to carry out its responsibilities under this section. The Civil Service Commission shall—

(1) be responsible for the annual review and approval of a national and regional equal employment opportunity plan which each department and agency and each appropriate unit referred to in subsection (a) of this section shall submit in order to maintain an affirmative program of equal employment opportunity for all such employees and applicants for employment;

(2) be responsible for the review and evaluation of the operation of all agency equal employment opportunity programs, periodically obtaining and publishing (on at least a semi-annual basis) progress reports from each such department, agency, or unit; and

(3) consult with and solicit the recommendations of interested individuals, groups, and organizations relating to equal employment opportunity.

The head of each such department, agency, or unit shall comply with such rules, regulations, orders, and instructions which shall include a provision that an employee or applicant for employment shall be notified of any final action taken on any complaint of discrimination filed by him thereunder.  The plan submitted by each department, agency, and unit shall include, but not be limited to—

(1) provisions for the establishment of training and education programs designed to provide a maximum opportunity for employees to advance so as to perform at their highest potential; and

(2) a description of the qualifications in terms of training and experience relating to equal employment opportunity for the principal and operating officials of each such department, agency, or unit responsible for carrying out the equal employment opportunity program and of the allocation of personnel and resources proposed by such department, agency, or unit to carry out its equal employment opportunity program.

With respect to employment in the Library of Congress, authorities granted in this subsection to the Civil Service Commission shall be exercised by the Librarian of Congress.

(c) Within thirty days of receipt of notice of final action taken by a department, agency, or unit referred to in subsection 717(a), or by the Civil Service Commission upon an appeal from a decision or order of such department, agency, or unit on a complaint of discrimination based on race, color, religion, sex or national origin, brought pursuant to subsection (a) of this section, Executive Order 11478 or any succeeding Executive orders, or after one hundred and eighty days from the filing of the initial charge with the department, agency, or unit or with the Civil Service Commission on appeal from a decision or order of such department, agency, or unit until such time as final action may be taken by a department, agency, or unit, an employee or applicant for employment, if aggrieved by the final disposition of his complaint, or by the failure to take final action on his complaint, may file a civil action as provided in section 706, in which civil action the head of the department, agency, or unit, as appropriate, shall be the defendant.*

(d) The provisions of section 706(f) through (k), as applicable, shall govern civil actions brought hereunder.

(e) Nothing contained in this Act shall relieve any Government agency or official of its or his primary responsibility to assure nondiscrimination in employment as required by the Constitution and statutes or of its or his responsibilities under Executive Order 11478 relating to equal employment opportunity in the Federal Government.

---

* All equal opportunity in federal employment enforcement and related functions vested in the Civil Service Commission pursuant to subsections (b) and (c) were transferred to the Equal Employment Opportunity Commission by Reorg. Plan No. 1 of 1978, § 3, 3 C.F.R. 321 (1978), *reprinted in* 5 U.S.C. App. at 1155 (1978), *and in* 92 Stat. 3781 (1978).

SPECIAL PROVISION WITH RESPECT TO DENIAL, TERMINATION,
AND SUSPENSION OF GOVERNMENT CONTRACTS

**Sec. 718.**   No Government contract, or portion thereof, with any
employer, shall be denied, withheld, terminated, or suspended, by any
agency or officer of the United States under any equal employment opportunity law or order, where such employer has an affirmative action plan which has previously been accepted by the Government for
the same facility within the past twelve months without first according such employer full hearing and adjudication under the provisions
of title 5, United States Code, section 554, and the following pertinent
sections: *Provided*, That if such employer has deviated substantially
from such previously agreed to affirmative action plan, this section
shall not apply: *Provided further*, That for the purposes of this section
an affirmative action plan shall be deemed to have been accepted by
the Government at the time the appropriate compliance agency has
accepted such plan unless within forty-five days thereafter the Office of Federal Contract Compliance has disapproved such plan.

## LEGISLATIVE NOTE

### THE EQUAL EMPLOYMENT OPPORTUNITY
### ACT OF 1972*

Eight years ago, Congress enacted Title VII of the Civil Rights
Act of 1964 (Public Law 88–352) in recognition of the need for federal
legislation to deal with the problem of employment discrimination.
The Act established the Equal Employment Opportunity Commission
(EEOC) as the primary federal agency responsible for administering
the Act.

**Court Actions by EEOC**

Under the 1964 law, EEOC did not have the authority to issue judicially enforceable orders to back up its findings of discrimination.
In prohibiting discrimination in employment based on race, religion,
color, sex or national origin, the 1964 Act limited the Commission's
enforcement authority to "informal methods of conference, conciliation, and persuasion."

As a consequence, unless the Department of Justice concluded
that a pattern or practice of resistance to Title VII was involved, the
burden of obtaining enforceable relief rested upon the individual victim of discrimination.  He was required to go into court as a private

* Reprinted by special permission from
  "The Equal Employment Opportunity
  Act of 1972," published 1972 by The
  Bureau of National Affairs, Inc., Wash-
  ington. D.C. 20037.

party, with the expense and time that entails, in order to obtain an enforceable order.

"This failure to grant the EEOC meaningful enforcement powers has proven to be a major flaw in the operation of Title VII," the Senate Labor Committee concluded. It noted that the victim of discrimination was left with a remedy that "is time consuming, burdensome, and all too often, financially prohibitive."

The failure of the voluntary conciliation approach is reflected in EEOC workload statistics, the Committee observed. Since its inception, the Commission has received 81,000 charges. Of this number, EEOC has been able to achieve a totally, or at least partially, satisfactory conciliation in less than half. Thus, in more than half of the cases, the aggrieved individual either had to give up his claim or, if he had the necessary funds and time, to pursue the case through the federal courts.

Under the 1972 amendments, the Commission, if it is unable to secure an acceptable conciliation agreement within 30 days after the filing of the charge or after the expiration of the state agency deferral period, may bring an action against the respondent in a U. S. district court. (In cases against a state or local government, the Attorney General, rather than EEOC, is authorized to bring the action.) The enforcement procedure under the 1972 Act is discussed in more detail below.

### Individual Actions

Where the Commission is not able to pursue a complaint with satisfactory speed, or enters into an agreement that is not acceptable to the aggrieved party, the 1972 law provides that the individual shall have an opportunity to seek his own court remedy.

If the Commission dismisses a charge, or, if within 180 days of the charge's filing EEOC has neither issued a complaint nor entered into a conciliation or settlement agreement that is acceptable to EEOC and the aggrieved party, it shall notify the aggrieved party, and he may bring an action in a U. S. district court on his own within the next 90 days. (See 705(b) (1) )

It is hoped and expected that recourse to this remedy will be the exception rather than the rule, and that the vast majority of complaints will be handled through the offices of the EEOC or the Attorney General. However, it was felt that the aggrieved person should be given a chance to escape the administrative process when he feels his claim has not been given adequate attention.

In such private actions, the courts are authorized at the complainant's request to appoint an attorney and to commence the action without payment of fees. EEOC (or the Attorney General in cases involving governmental entities) is authorized to intervene in these private actions if it is certified that the action is of general public importance.

## "Pattern or Practice" Authority

Under the 1964 law, the Attorney General was given authority to seek an injunction where he has reasonable cause to believe that individuals are engaged in a "pattern or practice of resistance" to the rights protected by Title VII. The new law provides for the transfer of this "pattern or practice" jurisdiction to the Commission two years after the enactment of the law. In the interim, the Commission and the Attorney General have concurrent jurisdiction in this area. The intent is to safeguard the "pattern or practice" power, while at the same time providing for a smooth and efficient transfer of that authority. (Sec. 707(c))

## Coverage: State & Local Governments

Under the 1964 law, state and local governments and their employees were excluded from coverage. The new law now includes all state and local governments, governmental agencies, political subdivisions (except for elected officials, their personal assistants, and immediate advisors) and the District of Columbia departments and agencies (except where subject by law to the federal competitive service). With this added authority, EEOC will be able to deal with the problem of discrimination in police forces, fire departments, and public schools, and other groups of public employees.

The exemption for elected officials and their personal assistants and immediate advisors "is intended to be construed very narrowly and is in no way intended to establish an overall narrowing of the expanded coverage of state and local governmental employees." (Sec. 701(a) and (f))

## Coverage: Federal Employees

While federal employees are not brought within the jurisdiction of EEOC, the 1972 amendments add a new section 717 making clear the obligation of the federal government to make all personnel actions free from discrimination based on race, color, sex, religion or national origin. The Civil Service Commission is given the authority under this provision to enforce equal employment opportunity in the federal government.

Federal employees and applicants for employment are given the same right as employees in private industry to bring court actions if they are dissatisfied with the government's handling of their complaint of bias. (Sec. 717)

## Coverage: Educational Institutions

The pre-existing exemption for employees of educational institutions is eliminated. It is estimated that this will bring within the jurisdiction of EEOC over 120,000 educational institutions, with approximately 2.8 million teachers and professional staff members and another 1.5 million non-professional staff members. (Sec. 701(b))

The special provision relating to religious educational institutions and other religious institutions was not eliminated. The exemption is from the ban on religious discrimination; such organizations remain subject to the provisions of Title VII with regard to race, color, sex, or national origin.

Under the 1964 Act, the exemption was limited to the religious activities of such institutions. Under the 1972 amendments, religious corporations, associations, educational institutions, or societies are permitted to employ individuals of a particular religion in all their activities, not just their religious activities. (Sec. 702)

## Coverage: Small Employers, Unions

Coverage of Title VII has been expanded to include employers of 15 or more persons and labor unions with 15 or more members. Since the Commission will be undertaking several new areas of responsibility under the proposed legislation, the legislators recognize that EEOC might have some difficulty in handling this increased caseload immediately. Therefore, the bill provides that the expansion take place one year after enactment. (Sec. 701(b) and (e))

## Coverage: Joint Labor-Management Committees

The list of unlawful employment practices is expanded in the 1972 amendments to include discrimination by joint labor-management committees that control apprenticeship or other training or retraining programs, including on-the-job training. The prohibition includes both discrimination in administering the program and in admission to the program. (Sec. 709(c))

## Religious Discrimination

A new section added by the 1972 amendments defines "religion" to include all aspects of religious observance, practice, and belief so as to require employers to make reasonable accommodations for employees whose "religion" may include observances, practices and beliefs such as sabbath observance, that differ from the employer's or potential employer's requirements regarding standards, schedules, or other business-related employment conditions.

Failure to make such accommodation is unlawful unless an employer can demonstrate that he cannot reasonably accommodate such beliefs, practices, or observances without undue hardship on the conduct of his business.   (Sec. 701(j))

\* \* \*

## Procedure in Absence of State EEO Law

Under the 1972 amendments (Sec. 705), the following procedures apply where no state equal employment opportunity law exists:

► A charge must be filed within 180 days after the occurrence of an alleged unlawful employment practice.   (The time limitation had been 90 days under the 1964 law.)

\* \* \*

► After a charge is filed, the Commission must serve a notice of the charge on the respondent within 10 days.   (New)

► The Commission must then investigate the charge after which it must make a determination whether there is reasonable cause to believe that the charge is true.   The Commission shall make its determination of reasonable cause as promptly as possible and, so far as practicable, within 120 days.   (No time limit specified in 1964 law.)

► If it finds no reasonable cause, the Commission must dismiss the charge;  if it finds reasonable cause, it will attempt to conciliate the case.   (Unchanged)

► If the Commission is unable to secure a conciliation agreement that is acceptable to the Commission, it may bring a civil action against any respondent in an appropriate U. S. district court.   In the case of a government agency, the Commission notifies the Attorney General who may bring a civil action.   A special master may be appointed if the district court has not assigned the case for trial within 120 days. (New)

► If the court finds that a respondent is engaging in an unlawful employment practice charged in the complaint, the court may enjoin the respondent from engaging in the unlawful employment practice and grant such affirmative relief as it may deem appropriate including, but not limited to, reinstatement with or without back pay.   Back pay is limited, however, to no more than that accrued during the two years prior to the filing of a charge with the Commission.   (Similar to court enforcement provisions under 1964 law that were available in private suits and "pattern or practice" suits.   Two-year limit on back pay is new.)

► In the event that the Commission dismisses a charge or if within 180 days from the filing of the charge, the Commission or the Attorney General has not filed a civil action or entered into a conciliation agreement to which the aggrieved person is a party, the Commission or the Attorney General will notify the aggrieved party.   Within 90 days after the receipt of such notice, the aggrieved person may bring a civil action against the respondent.   Should such a private action be brought, the Commission or the Attorney General (where a government agency is involved) may seek to intervene in the action. (Under the 1964 law, up to 90 days was allowed for obtaining a conciliation agreement, and the individual was given 30 days within which to bring suit.)

### Procedure with State EEO Law

Where a state equal employment opportunity law exists, the 1972 amendments specify this procedure:

▶ A charge must be filed within 180 days after the occurrence of an alleged unlawful employment practice. (90 days under 1964 law)

▶ If a charge is initially filed with a state or local agency, such charge must be filed with the Commission within 300 days after the alleged unlawful practice has occurred or within 30 days after receipt of notice that the state or local agency has terminated its proceedings. (Under the old law, the time limitations were 210 days after occurrence and 30 days after notice of termination of state proceedings.)

▶ Where a state or local EEO statute exists, the EEOC must wait 60 days after state or local proceedings have been commenced, unless those proceedings are terminated sooner, before it can act on a charge. The deferral period is extended to 120 days during the first year after enactment of a state or local proceeding. (Deferral time periods were the same under the 1964 law.)

▶ Once the deferral is concluded, the Commission must serve a notice of the charge on the respondent within 10 days. (Unchanged)

▶ The Commission then must investigate the charge, after which it must make a determination whether there is reasonable cause to believe that the charge is true. The Commission shall make its determination of reasonable cause as promptly as possible and, so far as practicable, within 120 days. It is required to accord substantial weight to the decision of state or local authorities. (The 120-day period is new, as is the provision on the weight to be accorded the state or local decision.)

The procedure from this point forward is the same as that followed in cases where there is no state or local EEO law.

\* \* \*

### Charge on Behalf of Victim

Under the 1964 law, a charge could be filed under oath by a person aggrieved or by a member of the Commission. EEOC held that this provision precluded organizations, such as unions or civil rights groups, from filing charges on behalf of victims of discrimination. Under the 1972 amendments, a charge also may be filed by or on behalf of a person aggrieved. This permits aggrieved persons to have charges processed in situations where they are unwilling to come forward publicly for fear of reprisal. (Sec. 705(b))

## Miscellaneous Changes

*General Counsel:* The 1972 Act calls for appointment by the President, subject to Senate confirmation of an EEOC General Counsel for a four-year term. The General Counsel will be responsible for the conduct of EEOC litigation and will concur with the EEOC Chairman on appointment and supervision of regional attorneys. (Sec. 705(b) (1))

\* \* \*

*Contract Denials, Suspensions:* Under a new provision added by the 1972 Act, no government contract with any employer may be denied, withheld, terminated, or suspended pursuant to any EEO law or order if the employer has an affirmative action plan that had been accepted by the government for the same facility within the past 12 months, without first giving the employer a full hearing and adjudication. The hearing and adjudication would not be required if the employer had substantially deviated from the affirmative action plan. (Sec. 718)

## Provisions Not Adopted

The Conference Committee excluded from the final version of the Act two provisions in the House bill that were an anathema to civil rights groups. The first would have prohibited EEOC from bringing class action suits on behalf of groups of workers. The second would have made EEOC the sole federal authority to combat job discrimination. Now, an aggrieved individual presumably will be able to seek relief through EEOC, under Title VII, the National Labor Relations Board under the Taft Act, the Office of Federal Contract Compliance under the Executive Orders on nondiscrimination by federal contractors, and the courts under the Civil Rights Act of 1866.

## CIVIL SERVICE REFORM ACT OF 1978
## TITLE VII—FEDERAL SERVICE LABOR–MANAGEMENT RELATIONS

92 Stat. 1191 (1978), as amended by 94 Stat. 2168 (1980),
98 Stat. 47 (1984); 5 U.S.C. §§ 7101–7135 (1982).

SUBCHAPTER I—GENERAL PROVISIONS

### Sec. 7101. Findings and purpose

(a) The Congress finds that —

(1) experience in both private and public employment indicates that the statutory protection of the right of employees to organize, bargain collectively, and participate through labor organizations of their own choosing in decisions which affect them —

(A) safeguards the public interest,

(B) contributes to the effective conduct of public business, and

(C) facilitates and encourages the amicable settlement of disputes between employees and their employers involving conditions of employment; and

(2) the public interest demands the highest standards of employee performance and the continued development and implementation of modern and progressive work practices to facilitate and improve employee performance and the efficient accomplishment of the operations of the Government.

Therefore, labor organizations and collective bargaining in the civil service are in the public interest.

(b) It is the purpose of this chapter to prescribe certain rights and obligations of the employees of the Federal Government and to establish procedures which are designed to meet the special requirements and needs of the Government. The provisions of this chapter should be interpreted in a manner consistent with the requirement of an effective and efficient government.

### Sec. 7102. Employees' rights

Each employee shall have the right to form, join, or assist any labor organization, or to refrain from any such activity, freely and without fear of penalty or reprisal, and each employee shall be protected in the exercise of such right. Except as otherwise provided under this chapter, such right includes the right —

(1) to act for a labor organization in the capacity of a representative and the right, in that capacity, to present the views of the labor organization to heads of agencies and other officials of the executive branch of the Government, the Congress, or other appropriate authorities, and

(2) to engage in collective bargaining with respect to conditions of employment through representatives chosen by employees under this chapter.

### Sec. 7103. Definitions; application

(a) For the purpose of this chapter —

(1) "person" means an individual, labor organization or agency;

(2) "employee" means an individual —

(A) employed in an agency; or

(B) whose employment in an agency has ceased because of any unfair labor practice under section 7116 of this title and who has not obtained any other regular and substantially equivalent employment, as determined under regulations prescribed by the Federal Labor Relations Authority;

but does not include —

(i) an alien or noncitizen of the United States who occupies a position outside the United States;

(ii) a member of the uniformed services;

(iii) a supervisor or a management official;

(iv) an officer or employee in the Foreign Service of the United States employed in the Department of State, the International Communication Agency, the United States International Development Cooperation Agency, the Department of Agriculture, or the Department of Commerce; or

(v) any person who participates in a strike in violation of section 7311 of this title;

(3) "agency" means an Executive agency (including a nonappropriated fund instrumentality described in section 2105(c) of this title and the Veterans' Canteen Service, Veterans' Administration), the Library of Congress, and the Government Printing Office, but does not include —

(A) the General Accounting Office;

(B) the Federal Bureau of Investigation;

(C) the Central Intelligence Agency;

(D) the National Security Agency;

(E) the Tennessee Valley Authority;

(F) the Federal Labor Relations Authority; or

(G) the Federal Service Impasses Panel;

(4) "labor organization" means an organization composed in whole or in part of employees, in which employees participate and pay dues, and which has as a purpose the dealing with an agency concerning grievances and conditions of employment, but does not include —

(A) an organization which, by its constitution, bylaws, tacit agreement among its members, or otherwise, denies membership because of race, color, creed, national origin, sex, age, preferential or nonpreferential civil service status, political affiliation, marital status, or handicapping condition;

(B) an organization which advocates the overthrow of the constitutional form of government of the United States;

(C) an organization sponsored by an agency; or

(D) an organization which participates in the conduct of a strike against the Government or any agency thereof or imposes a duty or obligation to conduct, assist, or participate in such a strike;

(5) "dues" means dues, fees, and assessments;

(6) "Authority" means the Federal Labor Relations Authority described in section 7104(a) of this title;

(7) "Panel" means the Federal Service Impasses Panel described in section 7119(c) of this title;

(8) "collective bargaining agreement" means an agreement entered into as a result of collective bargaining pursuant to the provisions of this chapter;

(9) "grievance" means any complaint —

(A) by any employee concerning any matter relating to the employment of the employee;

(B) by any labor organization concerning any matter relating to the employment of any employee; or

(C) by any employee, labor organization, or agency concerning —

(i) the effect or interpretation, or a claim of breach, of a collective bargaining agreement; or

(ii) any claimed violation, misinterpretation, or misapplication of any law, rule, or regulation affecting conditions of employment;

(10) "supervisor" means an individual employed by an agency having authority in the interest of the agency to hire, direct, assign, promote, reward, transfer, furlough, layoff, recall, suspend, discipline, or remove employees, to adjust their grievances, or to effectively recommend such action, if the exercise of the authority is not merely routine or clerical in nature but requires the consistent exercise of independent judgment, except that, with respect to any unit which includes firefighters or nurses, the term "supervisor" includes only those individuals who devote a preponderance of their employment time to exercising such authority;

(11) "management official" means an individual employed by an agency in a position the duties and responsibilities of which require or authorize the individual to formulate, determine, or influence the policies of the agency;

(12) "collective bargaining" means the performance of the mutual obligation of the representative of an agency and the exclusive representative of employees in an appropriate unit in the agency to meet at reasonable times and to consult and bargain in a good-faith effort to reach agreement with respect to the conditions of employment affecting such employees and to execute, if requested by either party, a written document incorporating any collective bargaining agreement reached, but the obligation referred to in this paragraph does not compel either party to agree to a proposal or to make a concession;

(13) "confidential employee" means an employee who acts in a confidential capacity with respect to an individual who formulates or effectuates management policies in the field of labor-management relations;

(14) "conditions of employment" means personnel policies, practices, and matters, whether established by rule, regulation, or otherwise, affecting working conditions, except that such term does not include policies, practices, and matters —

(A) relating to political activities prohibited under subchapter III of chapter 73 of this title;

(B) relating to the classification of any position; or

(C) to the extent such matters are specifically provided for by Federal statute;

(15) "professional employee" means —

(A) an employee engaged in the performance of work —

    (i) requiring knowledge of an advanced type in a field of science or learning customarily acquired by a prolonged course of specialized intellectual instruction and study in an institution of higher learning or a hospital (as distinguished from knowledge acquired by a general academic education, or from an apprenticeship, or from training in the performance of routine mental, manual, mechanical, or physical activities);

    (ii) requiring the consistent exercise of discretion and judgment in its performance;

    (iii) which is predominantly intellectual and varied in character (as distinguished from routine mental, manual, mechanical, or physical work); and

    (iv) which is of such character that the output produced or the result accomplished by such work cannot be standardized in relation to a given period of time; or

(B) an employee who has completed the courses of specialized intellectual instruction and study described in subparagraph (A)(i) of this paragraph and is performing related work under appropriate direction or guidance to qualify the employee as a professional employee described in subparagraph (A) of this paragraph;

(16) "exclusive representative" means any labor organization which —

(A) is certified as the exclusive representative of employees in an appropriate unit pursuant to section 7111 of this title; or

(B) was recognized by an agency immediately before the effective date of this chapter as the exclusive representative of employees in an appropriate unit—

    (i) on the basis of an election, or

    (ii) on any basis other than an election, and continues to be so recognized in accordance with the provisions of this chapter;

(17) "firefighter" means any employee engaged in the performance of work directly connected with the control and extinguish-

ment of fires or the maintenance and use of firefighting apparatus and equipment; and

(18) "United States" means the 50 States, the District of Columbia, the Commonwealth of Puerto Rico, Guam, the Virgin Islands, the Trust Territory of the Pacific Islands, and any territory or possession of the United States.

(b)(1) The President may issue an order excluding any agency or subdivision thereof from coverage under this chapter if the President determines that —

(A) the agency or subdivision has as a primary function intelligence, counterintelligence, investigative, or national security work, and

(B) the provisions of this chapter cannot be applied to that agency or subdivision in a manner consistent with national security requirements and considerations.

(2) The President may issue an order suspending any provision of this chapter with respect to any agency, installation, or activity located outside the 50 States and the District of Columbia, if the President determines that the suspension is necessary in the interest of national security.

### Sec. 7104. Federal Labor Relations Authority

(a) The Federal Labor Relations Authority is composed of three members, not more than 2 of whom may be adherents of the same political party. No member shall engage in any other business or employment or hold another office or position in the Government of the United States except as otherwise provided by law.

(b) Members of the Authority shall be appointed by the President by and with the advice and consent of the Senate, and may be removed by the President only upon notice and hearing and only for inefficiency, neglect of duty, or malfeasance in office. The President shall designate one member to serve as chairman of the Authority. The Chairman is the chief executive and administrative officer of the Authority.

(c) A member of the Authority shall be appointed for a term of 5 years. An individual chosen to fill a vacancy shall be appointed for the unexpired term of the member replaced. The term of any member shall not expire before the earlier of—

(1) the date on which the member's successor takes office, or

(2) the last day of the Congress beginning after the date on which the member's term of office would (but for this paragraph) expire.

(d) A vacancy in the Authority shall not impair the right of the remaining members to exercise all of the powers of the Authority.

(e) The Authority shall make an annual report to the President for transmittal to the Congress which shall include information as to the cases it has heard and the decisions it has rendered.

(f)(1) The General Counsel of the Authority shall be appointed by the President, by and with the advice and consent of the Senate, for a term of 5 years.

The General Counsel may be removed at any time by the President. The General Counsel shall hold no other office or position in the Government of the United States except as provided by law.

(2) The General Counsel may —

(A) investigate alleged unfair labor practices under this chapter,

(B) file and prosecute complaints under this chapter, and

(C) exercise such other powers of the Authority as the Authority may prescribe.

(3) The General Counsel shall have direct authority over, and responsibility for, all employees in the office of General Counsel, including employees of the General Counsel in the regional offices of the Authority.

## Sec. 7105. Powers and duties of the Authority

(a)(1) The Authority shall provide leadership in establishing policies and guidance relating to matters under this chapter, and, except as otherwise provided, shall be responsible for carrying out the purpose of this chapter.

(2) The Authority shall, to the extent provided in this chapter and in accordance with regulations prescribed by the Authority —

(A) determine the appropriateness of units for labor organization representation under section 7112 of this title;

(B) supervise or conduct elections to determine whether a labor organization has been selected as an exclusive representative by a majority of the employees in an appropriate unit and otherwise administer the provisions of section 7111 of this title relating to the according of exclusive recognition to labor organizations;

(C) prescribe criteria and resolve issues relating to the granting of national consultation rights under section 7113 of this title;

(D) prescribe criteria and resolve issues relating to determining compelling need for agency rules or regulations under section 7117(b) of this title;

(E) resolve issues relating to the duty to bargain in good faith under section 7117(c) of this title;

(F) prescribe criteria relating to the granting of consultation rights with respect to conditions of employment under section 7117(d) of this title;

(G) conduct hearings and resolve complaints of unfair labor practices under section 7118 of this title;

(H) resolve exceptions to arbitrator's awards under section 7122 of this title; and

(I) take such other actions as are necessary and appropriate to effectively administer the provisions of this chapter.

(b) The Authority shall adopt an official seal which shall be judicially noticed.

(c) The principal office of the Authority shall be in or about the District of Columbia, but the Authority may meet and exercise any or all of its powers at any time or place.  Except as otherwise expressly provided by law, the Authority may, by one or more of its members or by such agents as it may designate, make any appropriate inquiry necessary to carry out its duties wherever persons subject to this chapter are located.  Any member who participates in the inquiry shall not be disqualified from later participating in a decision of the Authority in any case relating to the inquiry.

(d) The Authority shall appoint an Executive Director and such regional directors, administrative law judges under section 3105 of this title, and other individuals as it may from time to time find necessary for the proper performance of its functions.

(e)(1) The Authority may delegate to any regional director its authority under this chapter —

(A) to determine whether a group of employees is an appropriate unit;

(B) to conduct investigations and to provide for hearings;

(C) to determine whether a question of representation exists and to direct an election; and

(D) to supervise or conduct secret ballot elections and certify the results thereof.

(2) The Authority may delegate to any administrative law judge appointed under subsection (d) of this section its authority under section 7118 of this title to determine whether any person has engaged in or is engaging in an unfair labor practice.  The Authority may delegate to officers and employees appointed under subsection (d) authority to perform such duties and make such expenditures as may be necessary.

(f) If the Authority delegates any authority to any regional director or administrative law judge to take any action pursuant to subsection (c) of this section, the Authority may, upon application by any interested person filed within 60 days after the date of the action, review such action, but the review shall not, unless specifically ordered by the Authority, operate as a stay of action.  The Authority may affirm, modify, or reverse any action reviewed under this subsection.  If the Authority does not undertake to grant review of the action under this subsection within 60 days after the later of —

(1) the date of the action; or

(2) the date of the filing of any application under this subsection for review of the action;

the action shall become the action of the Authority at the end of such 60-day period.

(g) In order to carry out its functions under this chapter, the Authority may —

(1) hold hearings;

(2) administer oaths, take the testimony or deposition of any person under oath, and issue subpoenas as provided in section 7133 of this title; and

(3) may require an agency or a labor organization to cease and desist from violations of this chapter and require it to take any remedial action it considers appropriate to carry out the policies of this chapter.

(h) Except as provided in section 518 of title 28, relating to litigation before the Supreme Court, attorneys designated by the Authority may appear for the Authority and represent the Authority in any civil action brought in connection with any function carried out by the authority pursuant to this title or as otherwise authorized by law.

(i) In the exercise of the functions of the Authority under this title, the Authority may request from the Director of the Office of Personnel Management an advisory opinion concerning the proper interpretation of rules, regulations, or policy directives issued by the Office of Personnel Management in connection with any matter before the Authority.

## Sec. 7106. Management rights

(a) Subject to subsection (b) of this section, nothing in this chapter shall affect the authority of any management official of any agency —

(1) to determine the mission, budget, organization, number of employees, and internal security practices of the agency; and

(2) in accordance with applicable laws —

(A) to hire, assign, direct, layoff, and retain employees in the agency, or to suspend, remove, reduce in grade or pay, or take other disciplinary action against such employees;

(B) to assign work, to make determinations with respect to contracting out, and to determine the personnel by which agency operations shall be conducted;

(C) with respect to filling positions, to make selections for appointments from—

(i) among properly ranked and certified candidates for promotion; or

(ii) any other appropriate source; and

(D) to take whatever actions may be necessary to carry out the agency mission during emergencies.

(b) Nothing in this section shall preclude any agency and any labor organization from negotiating —

(1) at the election of the agency, on the numbers, types, and grades of employees or positions assigned to any organizational subdivision,

work project, or tour of duty, or on the technology, methods, and means of performing work;

(2) procedures which management officials of the agency will observe in exercising any authority under this section; or

(3) appropriate arrangements for employees adversely affected by the exercise of any authority under this section by such management officials.

## SUBCHAPTER II — RIGHTS AND DUTIES OF AGENCIES AND LABOR ORGANIZATIONS

### Sec. 7111. Executive recognition of labor organizations

(a) An agency shall accord exclusive recognition to a labor organization if the organization has been selected as the representative, in a secret ballot election, by a majority of the employees in an appropriate unit who cast valid ballots in the election.

(b) If a petition is filed with the Authority —

(1) by any person alleging —

(A) in the case of an appropriate unit for which there is no exclusive representative, that 30 percent of the employees in the appropriate unit wish to be represented for the purpose of collective bargaining by an exclusive representative, or

(B) in the case of an appropriate unit for which there is an exclusive representative, that 30 percent of the employees in the unit allege that the exclusive representative is no longer the representative of the majority of the employees in the unit; or

(2) by any person seeking clarification of, or an amendment to, a certification then in effect or a matter relating to representation;

the Authority shall investigate the petition, and if it has reasonable cause to believe that a question of representation exists, it shall provide an opportunity for a hearing (for which a transcript shall be kept) after reasonable notice. If the Authority finds on the record of the hearing that a question of representation exists, the Authority shall conduct an election on the question by secret ballot and shall certify the results thereof. An election under this subsection shall not be conducted in any appropriate unit or in any subdivision thereof within which, in the preceding 12 calendar months, a valid election under this subsection has been held.

(c) A labor organization which —

(1) has been designated by at least 10 percent of the employees in the unit specified in any petition filed pursuant to subsection (b) of this section;

(2) has submitted a valid copy of a current or recently expired collective bargaining agreement for the unit; or

(3) has submitted other evidence that it is the exclusive representative of the employees involved;

may intervene with respect to a petition filed pursuant to subsection (b) of this section and shall be placed on the ballot of any election under such subsection (b) with respect to the petition.

(d) The Authority shall determine who is eligible to vote in any election under this section and shall establish rules governing any such election, which shall include rules allowing employees eligible to vote the opportunity to choose —

(1) from labor organizations on the ballot, that labor organization which the employees wish to have represent them; or

(2) not to be represented by a labor organization.

In any election in which no choice on the ballot receives a majority of the votes cast, a runoff election shall be conducted between the two choices receiving the highest number of votes. A labor organization which receives the majority of the votes cast in an election shall be certified by the Authority as the exclusive representative.

(e) A labor organization seeking exclusive recognition shall submit to the Authority and the agency involved a roster of its officers and representatives, a copy of its constitution and bylaws, and a statement of its objectives.

(f) Exclusive recognition shall not be accorded to a labor organization —

(1) if the Authority determines that the labor organization is subject to corrupt influences or influences opposed to democratic principles;

(2) in the case of a petition filed pursuant to subsection (b)(1)(A) of this section, if there is not credible evidence that at least 30 percent of the employees in the unit specified in the petition wish to be represented for the purpose of collective bargaining by the labor organization seeking exclusive recognition;

(3) if there is then in effect a lawful written collective bargaining agreement between the agency involved and an exclusive representative (other than the labor organization seeking exclusive recognition) covering any employees included in the unit specified in the petition, unless —

(A) the collective bargaining agreement has been in effect for more than 3 years, or

(B) the petition for exclusive recognition is filed not more than 105 days and not less than 60 days before the expiration date of the collective bargaining agreement; or

(4) if the Authority has, within the previous 12 calendar months, conducted a secret ballot election for the unit described in any petition under this section and in such election a majority of the employees voting chose a labor organization for certification as the unit's exclusive representative.

(g) Nothing in this section shall be construed to prohibit the waiving of hearings by stipulation for the purpose of a consent election in conformity with regulations and rules or decisions of the Authority.

### Sec. 7112. Determination of appropriate units for labor organization representation

(a)(1) The Authority shall determine the appropriateness of any unit. The Authority shall determine in each case whether, in order to ensure employees the fullest freedom in exercising the rights guaranteed under this chapter, the appropriate unit should be established on an agency, plant, installation, functional, or other basis and shall determine any unit to be an appropriate unit only if the determination will ensure a clear and identifiable community of interest among the employees in the unit and will promote effective dealings with, and efficiency of the operations of, the agency involved.

(b) A unit shall not be determined to be appropriate under this section solely on the basis of the extent to which employees in the proposed unit have organized, nor shall a unit be determined to be appropriate if it includes —

(1) except as provided under section 7135(a)(2) of this title, any management official or supervisor;

(2) a confidential employee;

(3) an employee engaged in personnel work in other than a purely clerical capacity;

(4) an employee engaged in administering the provisions of this chapter;

(5) both professional employees and other employees, unless a majority of the professional employees vote for inclusion in the unit;

(6) any employee engaged in intelligence, counterintelligence, investigative, or security work which directly affects national security; or

(7) any employee primarily engaged in investigation or audit functions relating to the work of individuals employed by an agency whose duties directly affect the internal security of the agency, but only if the functions are undertaken to ensure that the duties are discharged honestly and with integrity.

(c) Any employee who is engaged in administering any provision of law relating to labor-management relations may not be represented by a labor organization —

(1) which represents other individuals to whom such provision applies; or

(2) which is affiliated directly or indirectly with an organization which represents other individuals to whom such provision applies.

(d) Two or more units which are in an agency and for which a labor organization is the exclusive representative may, upon petition by the agency or labor organization, be consolidated with or without an election into a single larger unit if the Authority considers the larger unit to be appropriate. The Authority shall certify the labor organization as the exclusive representative of the new larger unit.

### Sec. 7113.  National consultation rights

(a)(1) If, in connection with any agency, no labor organization has been accorded exclusive recognition on an agency basis, a labor organization which is the exclusive representative of a substantial number of the employees of the agency, as determined in accordance with criteria prescribed by the Authority, shall be granted national consultation rights by the agency.  National consultation rights shall terminate when the labor organization no longer meets the criteria prescribed by the Authority.  Any issue relating to any labor organization's eligibility for, or continuation of, national consultation rights shall be subject to determination by the Authority.

(b)(1) Any labor organization having national consultation rights in connection with any agency under subsection (a) of this section shall —

(A) be informed of any substantive change in conditions of employment proposed by the agency, and

(B) be permitted reasonable time to present its views and recommendations regarding the changes.

(2) If any views or recommendations are presented under paragraph (1) of this subsection to an agency by any labor organization —

(A) the agency shall consider the views or recommendations before taking final action on any matter with respect to which the views or recommendations are presented; and

(B) the agency shall provide the labor organization a written statement of the reasons for taking the final action.

(c) Nothing in this section shall be construed to limit the right of any agency or exclusive representative to engage in collective bargaining.

### Sec. 7114.  Representation rights and duties

(a)(1) A labor organization which has been accorded exclusive recognition is the exclusive representative of the employees in the unit it represents and is entitled to act for, and negotiate collective bargaining agreements covering, all employees in the unit.  An exclusive representative is responsible for representing the interests of all employees in the unit it represents without discrimination and without regard to labor organization membership.

(2) An exclusive representative of an appropriate unit in an agency shall be given the opportunity to be represented at —

(A) any formal discussion between one or more representatives of the agency and one or more employees in the unit or their representatives concerning any grievance or any personnel policy or practices or other general condition of employment; or

(B) any examination of an employee in the unit by a representative of the agency in connection with an investigation if —

(i) the employee reasonably believes that the examination

may result in disciplinary action against the employee; and

(ii) the employee requests representation.

(3) Each agency shall annually inform its employees of their rights under paragraph (2)(B) of this subsection.

(4) Any agency and any exclusive representative in any appropriate unit in the agency, through appropriate representatives, shall meet and negotiate in good faith for the purposes of arriving at a collective bargaining agreement. In addition, the agency and the exclusive representative may determine appropriate techniques, consistent with the provisions of section 7119 of this title, to assist in any negotiation.

(5) The rights of an exclusive representative under the provisions of this subsection shall not be construed to preclude an employee from —

(A) being represented by an attorney or other representative, other than the exclusive representative, of the employee's own choosing in any grievance or appeal action; or

(B) exercising grievance or appellate rights established by law, rule, or regulation; except in the case of grievance or appeal provisions negotiated by this chapter.

(b) The duty of an agency and an exclusive representative to negotiate in good faith under subsection (a) of this section shall include the obligation —

(1) to approach the negotiations with a sincere resolve to reach a collective bargaining agreement;

(2) to be represented at the negotiations by duly authorized representatives prepared to discuss and negotiate on any conditions of employment;

(3) to meet at reasonable times and convenient places as frequently as may be necessary, and to avoid unnecessary delays;

(4) in the case of an agency, to furnish to the exclusive representative involved, or its authorized representative, upon request and, to the extent not prohibited by law, data —

(A) which is normally maintained by the agency in the regular course of business;

(B) which is reasonably available and necessary for full and proper discussion, understanding, and negotiation of subjects within the scope of collective bargaining; and

(C) which does not constitute guidance, advice, counsel, or training provided for management officials or supervisors, relating to collective bargaining; and

(5) if agreement is reached, to execute on the request of any party to the negotiation a written document embodying the agreed terms, and to take steps as are necessary to implement such agreement.

(c)(1) An agreement between any agency and an exclusive representative shall be subject to approval by the head of the agency.

(2) The head of the agency shall approve the agreement within 30 days from the date the agreement is executed if the agreement is in accordance with the provisions of this chapter and any other applicable

law, rule, or regulation (unless the agency has granted an exception to the provision).

(3) If the head of the agency does not approve or disapprove the agreement within the 30-day period, the agreement shall take effect and shall be binding on the agency and the exclusive representative subject to the provisions of this chapter and any other applicable law, rule, or regulation.

(4) A local agreement subject to a national or other controlling agreement at a high level shall be approved under the procedures of the controlling agreement or, if none, under regulations prescribed by the agency.

### Sec. 7115. Allotments to representatives

(a) If an agency has received from an employee in an appropriate unit a written assignment which authorizes the agency to deduct from the pay of the employee amounts for the payment or regular and periodic dues of the exclusive representative of the unit, the agency shall honor the assignment and make an appropriate allotment pursuant to the assignment. Any such allotment shall be made at no cost to the exclusive representative or the employee. Except as provided under subsection (b) of this section, any such assignment may not be revoked for a period of 1 year.

(b) An allotment under subsection (a) of this section for the deduction of dues with respect to any employee shall terminate when —

(1) the agreement between the agency and the exclusive representative involved ceases to be applicable to the employee; or

(2) the employee is suspended or expelled from the membership in the exclusive representative.

(c)(1) Subject to paragraph (2) of this subsection, if a petition has been filed with the Authority by a labor organization alleging that 10 percent of the employees in an appropriate unit in an agency have membership in the labor organization, the Authority shall investigate the petition to determine its validity. Upon certification by the Authority of the validity of the petition, the agency shall have a duty to negotiate with the labor organization solely concerning the deduction of dues of the labor organization from the pay of the members of the labor organization who are employees in the unit and who make a voluntary allotment for such purpose.

(2)(A) The provisions of paragraph (1) of this subsection shall not apply in the case of any appropriate unit for which there is an exclusive representative.

(B) Any agreement under paragraph (1) of this subsection between a labor organization and an agency with respect to an appropriate unit shall be null and void upon the certification of an exclusive representative of the unit.

### Sec. 7116. Unfair labor practices

(a) For the purpose of this chapter, it shall be an unfair labor practice for an agency —

(1) to interfere with, restrain, or coerce any employee in the exercise by the employee of any right under this chapter;

(2) to encourage or discourage membership in any labor organization by discrimination in connection with hiring, tenure, promotion, or other conditions of employment;

(3) to sponsor, control, or otherwise assist any labor organization, other than to furnish, upon request, customary and routine services and facilities if the services and facilities are also furnished on an impartial basis to other labor organizations having equivalent status;

(4) to discipline or otherwise discriminate against an employee because the employee has filed a complaint, affidavit, or petition, or has given any information or testimony under the chapter;

(5) to refuse to consult or negotiate in good faith with a labor organization as required by this chapter;

(6) to fail or refuse to cooperate in impasse procedures and impasse decisions as required by this chapter;

(7) to enforce any rule or regulation (other than a rule or regulation implementing section 2302 of this title) which is in conflict with any applicable collective bargaining agreement if the agreement was in effect before the date the rule or regulation was prescribed; or

(8) to otherwise fail or refuse to comply with any provision of this chapter.

(b) For the purpose of this chapter, it shall be an unfair labor practice for a labor organization —

(1) to interfere with, restrain, or coerce any employee in the exercise by the employee of any right under this chapter;

(2) to cause or attempt to cause an agency to discriminate against any employee in the exercise by the employee of any right under this chapter;

(3) to coerce, discipline, fine, or attempt to coerce a member of the labor organization as punishment, reprisal, or for the purpose of hindering or impeding the member's work performance or productivity as an employee or the discharge of the member's duties as an employee;

(4) to discriminate against an employee with regards to the terms or conditions of membership in the labor organization on the basis of race, color, creed, national origin, sex, age, preferential or nonpreferential civil service status, political affiliation, martial status, or handicapping condition;

(5) to refuse to consult or negotiate in good faith with an agency as required by this chapter;

(6) to fail or refuse to cooperate in impasse procedures and impasse decisions as required by this chapter;

(7)(A) to call, or participate in, a strike, work stoppage, or slow-down, or picketing of an agency in a labor-management dispute if such picketing interferes with an agency's operation or

(B) to condone any activity described in subparagraph (A) of this paragraph by failing to take action to prevent or stop such activity; or

(8) to otherwise fail or refuse to comply with any provision of this chapter. Nothing in paragraph (7) of this subsection shall result in any informational picketing which does not interfere with an agency's operations being considered as an unfair labor practice.

(c) For the purpose of this chapter it shall be an unfair labor practice for an exclusive representative to deny membership to any employee in the appropriate unit represented by such exclusive representative except for failure —

(1) to meet reasonable occupational standards uniformly required for admission, or

(2) to tender dues uniformly required as a condition of acquiring and retaining membership.
This subsection does not preclude any labor organization from enforcing discipline in accordance with procedures under its constitution or bylaws to the extent consistent with the provisions of this chapter.

(d) Issues which can properly be raised under an appeals procedure may not be raised as unfair labor practices prohibited under this section. Except for matters wherein, under sections 7121 (e) and (f) of this title, an employee has an option of using the negotiated grievance procedure or an appeals procedure, issues which can be raised under a grievance procedure may, in the discretion of the aggrieved party, be raised under the grievance procedure or as an unfair labor practice under this section, but not under both procedures.

(e) The expression of any personal view, argument, opinion or the making of any statement which —

(1) publicizes the fact of a representational election and encourages employees to exercise their right to vote in such election,

(2) corrects the record with respect to any false or misleading statement made by any person, or

(3) informs employees of the Government's policy relating to labor-management relations and representation,
shall not if the expression contains no threat of reprisal or force or promise of benefit or was made under coercive conditions, (A) constitute an unfair labor practice under any provision of this chapter, or (B) constitute grounds for the setting aside of any election conducted under any provision of this chapter.

### Sec. 7117. Duty to bargain in good faith; compelling need; duty to consult

(a)(1) Subject to paragraph (2) of this subsection, the duty to bargain in good faith shall, to the extent not inconsistent with any Federal law or any Government-wide rule or regulation, extend to matters which are the subject of any rule or regulation only if the rule or regulation is not a Government-wide rule or regulation.

(2) The duty to bargain in good faith shall, to the extent not inconsistent with Federal law or any Government-wide rule or regulation, extend to matters which are the subject of any agency rule or regulation referred to in paragraph (3) of this subsection only if the Authority has determined under subsection (b) of this section that no compelling need (as determined under regulations prescribed by the Authority) exists for the rule or regulation.

(3) Paragraph (2) of the subsection applies to any rule or regulation issued by any agency or issued by any primary national subdivision of such agency, unless an exclusive representative represents an appropriate unit including not less than a majority of the employees in the issuing agency or primary national subdivision, as the case may be, to whom the rule or regulation is applicable.

(b)(1) In any case of collective bargaining in which an exclusive representative alleges that no compelling need exists for any rule or regulation referred to in subsection (a)(3) of this section which is then in effect and which governs any matters at issue in such collective bargaining, the Authority shall determine under paragraph (2) of this subsection, in accordance with regulations prescribed by the Authority, whether such a compelling need exists.

(2) For the purpose of this section, a compelling need shall be determined not to exist for any rule or regulation only if —

(A) the agency, or primary national subdivision, as the case may be, which issued the rule or regulation informs the Authority in writing that a compelling need for the rule or regulation does not exist; or

(B) the Authority determines that a compelling need for a rule or regulation does not exist.

(3) A hearing may be held, in the discretion of the Authority, before a determination is made under this subsection.  If a hearing is held, it shall be expedited to the extent practicable and shall not include the General Counsel as a party.

(4) The agency, or primary national subdivision, as the case may be, which issued the rule or regulation shall be a necessary party at any hearing under this subsection.

(c)(1) Except in any case to which subsection (b) of this section applies, if an agency involved in collective bargaining with an exclusive representative alleges that the duty to bargain in good faith does not extend to any matter, the exclusive representative may appeal the allegation to the Authority in accordance with the provisions of this subsection.

(2) The exclusive representative may, on or before the 15th day after the date on which the agency first makes the allegation referred to in paragraph (1) of this subsection, institute an appeal under this subsection by —

(A) filing a petition with the Authority; and

(B) furnishing a copy of the petition to the head of the agency.

(3) On or before the 30th day after the date of the receipt by the head of the agency of the copy of the petition under paragraph (2)(B) of this subsection, the agency shall —

(A) file with the Authority a statement —

(i) withdrawing the allegation; or

(ii) setting forth in full its reasons supporting the allegation; and

(B) furnish a copy of such statement to the exclusive representative.

(4) On or before the 15th day after the date of the receipt by the exclusive representative of a copy of a statement under paragraph (3)(B) of this subsection, the exclusive representative shall file with the Authority its response to the statement.

(5) A hearing may be held, in the discretion of the Authority, before a determination is made under this subsection. If a hearing is held, it shall not include the General Counsel as a party.

(6) The Authority shall expedite proceedings under this subsection to the extent practicable and shall issue to the exclusive representative and to the agency a written decision on the allegation and specific reasons therefor at the earliest practicable date.

(d)(1) A labor organization which is the exclusive representative of a substantial number of employees, determined in accordance with criteria prescribed by the Authority, shall be granted consultation rights by any agency with respect to any Government-wide rule or regulation issued by the agency effecting any substantive change in any condition of employment. Such consultation rights shall terminate when the labor organization no longer meets the criteria prescribed by the Authority. Any issue relating to a labor organization's eligibility for, or continuation of, such consultation rights shall be subject to determination by the Authority.

(2) A labor organization having consultation rights under paragraph (1) of this subsection shall —

(A) be informed of any substantive change in conditions of employment proposed by the agency, and

(B) shall be permitted reasonable time to present its views and recommendations regarding the changes.

(3) If any views or recommendations are presented under paragraph (2) of this subsection to an agency by any labor organization —

(A) the agency shall consider the views or recommendations before taking final action on any matter with respect to which the views or recommendations are presented; and

(B) the agency shall provide the labor organization a written statement of the reasons for taking the final action.

### Sec. 7118. **Prevention of unfair labor practices**

(a)(1) If any agency or labor organization is charged by any person with having engaged in or engaging in an unfair labor practice, the General Counsel shall investigate the charge and may issue and cause to be served upon the agency or labor organization a complaint. In any case in which the General Counsel does not issue a complaint because the charge fails to state an unfair labor practice, the General Counsel shall provide the person making the charge a written statement of the reasons for not issuing a complaint.

(2) Any complaint under paragraph (1) of this subsection shall contain a notice —

(A) of the charge;

(B) that a hearing will be held before the Authority (or any member thereof or before an individual employed by the Authority and designated for such purpose); and

(C) of the time and place fixed for the hearing.

(3) The labor organization or agency involved shall have the right to file an answer to the original and any amended complaint and to appear in person or otherwise and give testimony at the time and place fixed in the complaint for the hearing.

(4)(A) Except as provided in subparagraph (B) of this paragraph, no complaint shall be issued based on any alleged unfair labor practice which occurred more than 6 months before the filing of the charge with the Authority.

(B) If the General Counsel determines that the person filing any charge was prevented from filing the charge during the 6-month period referred to in subparagraph (A) of this paragraph by reason of —

(i) any failure of the agency or labor organization against which the charge is made to perform a duty owed to the person, or

(ii) any concealment which prevented discovery of the alleged unfair labor practice duing the 6-month period, the General Counsel may issue a complaint based on the charge if the charge was filed during the 6-month period beginning on the day of the discovery by the person of the alleged unfair labor practice.

(5) The General Counsel may prescribe regulations providing for informal methods by which the alleged unfair labor practice may be resolved prior to the issuance of a complaint.

(6) The Authority (or any member thereof or any individual employed by the Authority and designated for such purpose) shall conduct a hearing on the complaint not earlier than 5 days after the date on which the complaint is served. In the discretion of the individual or individuals conducting the hearing, any person involved may be allowed to intervene in the hearing and to present testimony. Any such hearing shall, to the extent practicable, be conducted in accordance with the

provisions of subchapter II of chapter 5 of this title, except that the parties shall not be bound by rules of evidence, whether statutory, common law, or adopted by a court. A transcript shall be kept of the hearing. After such a hearing the Authority, in its discretion, may upon notice receive further evidence or hear argument.

(7) If the Authority (or any member thereof or any individual employed by the Authority and designated for such purpose) determines after any hearing on a complaint under paragraph (5) of this subsection that the preponderance of the evidence received demonstrates that the agency or labor organization named in the complaint has engaged in or is engaging in an unfair labor practice, then the individual or individuals conducting the hearing shall state in writing their findings of fact and shall issue and cause to be served on the agency or labor organization an order —

(A) to cease and desist from any such unfair labor practice in which the agency or labor organization is engaged;

(B) requiring the parties to renegotiate a collective bargaining agreement in accordance with the order of the Authority and requiring that the agreement as amended, be given retroactive effect;

(C) requiring reinstatement of an employee with backpay in accordance with section 5596 of this title; or

(D) including any combination of the actions described in subparagraphs (A) through (C) of this paragraph or such other action as will carry out the purpose of this chapter. If any such order requires reinstatement of an employee with backpay, backpay may be required of the agency (as provided in section 5596 of this title) or of the labor organization, as the case may be, which is found to have engaged in the unfair labor practice involved.

(8) If the individual or individuals conducting the hearing determine that the preponderance of the evidence received fails to demonstrate that the agency or labor organization named in the complaint has engaged in or is engaging in an unfair labor practice, the individual or individuals shall state in writing their findings of fact and shall issue an order dismissing the complaint.

(b) In connection with any matter before the Authority in any proceeding under this section, the Authority may request, in accordance with the provisions of section 7105(i) of this title, from the director of the Office of Personnel Management an advisory opinion concerning the proper interpretation of rules, regulations, or other policy directives issued by the Office of Personnel Management.

### Sec. 7119. Negotiation Impasses;  Federal Service Impasses Panel

(a) The Federal Mediation and Conciliation Service shall provide services and assistance to agencies and exclusive representatives in the resolution of negotiation impasses. The Service shall determine under what circumstances and in what manner it shall provide services and assistance.

(b) If voluntary arrangements, including the services of the Federal Mediation and Conciliation Service or any other third-party mediation, fail to resolve a negotiation impasse —

(1) either party may request the Federal Service Impasses Panel to consider the matter, or

(2) the parties may agree to adopt a procedure for binding arbitration of the negotiated impasse, but only if the procedure is approved by the Panel.

(c)(1) The Federal Service Impasses Panel is an entity within the Authority, the function of which is to provide assistance in resolving negotiation impasses between agencies and exclusive representatives.

(2) The Panel shall be composed of a Chairman and at least six other members, who shall be appointed by the President solely on the basis of fitness to perform the duties and functions involved, from among individuals who are familiar with Government operations and knowledgeable in labor-management relations.

(3) Of the original members of the Panel, 2 members shall be appointed for a term of 1 year, 2 members shall be appointed for a term of 3 years, and the Chairman and the remaining members shall be appointed for a term of 5 years. Thereafter each member shall be appointed for a term of 5 years, except that an individual chosen to fill a vacancy shall be appointed for the unexpired term of the member replaced. Any member of the Panel may be removed by the President.

(4) The Panel may appoint an Executive Director and any other individuals it may from time to time find necessary for the proper performance of its duties. Each member of the Panel who is not an employee (as defined in section 2105 of this title) is entitled to pay at a rate equal to the daily equivalent of the maximum annual rate of basic pay then currently paid under the General Schedule for each day he is engaged in the performance of official business of the Panel, including travel time, and is entitled to travel expenses as provided under section 5703 of this title.

(5)(A) The Panel or its designee shall promptly investigate any impasse presented to it under subsection (b) of this section. The Panel shall consider the impasse and shall either —

(i) recommend to the parties procedures for the resolution of the impasse; or

(ii) assist the parties in resolving through whatever methods and procedures, including factfinding and recommendations, it may consider appropriate to accomplish the purpose of this section.

(B) If the parties do not arrive at a settlement after assistance by the Panel under subparagraph (A) of this paragraph, the Panel may —

(i) hold hearings;

(ii) administer oaths, take the testimony or deposition of any person under oath, and issue subpoenas as provided in section 7133 of this title; and

(iii) take whatever action is necessary and not inconsistent with this chapter to resolve the impasse.

(C) Notice of any final action of the Panel under this section shall be promptly served upon the parties, and the action shall be binding on such parties during the terms of the agreement, unless the parties agree otherwise.

### Sec. 7120. Standards of conduct for labor organizations

(a) An agency shall only accord recognition to a labor organization that is free from corrupt influences and influences opposed to basic democratic principles.  Except as provided in subsection (b) of this section, an organization is not required to prove that it is free from such influences if it is subject to governing requirements adopted by the organization or by a national or international labor organization or federation of labor organizations with which it is affiliated, or in which it participates, containing explicit and detailed provisions to which it subscribes calling for —

(1) the maintenance of democratic procedures and practices including provisions for periodic elections to be conducted subject to recognized safeguards and provisions defining and securing the right of individual members to participate in the affairs of the organization, to receive fair and equal treatment under the governing rules of the organization, and to receive fair process in disciplinary proceedings;

(2) the exclusion from office in the organization of persons affiliated with communist or other totalitarian movements and persons identified with corrupt influences;

(3) the prohibition of business or financial interests on the part of organization officers and agents which conflict with their duty to the organization and its members; and

(4) the maintenance of fiscal integrity in the conduct of the affairs of the organization, including provisions for accounting and financial controls and regular financial reports or summaries to be made available to members.

(b) Notwithstanding the fact that a labor organization has adopted or subscribed to standards of conduct as provided in subsection (a) of this section, the organization is required to furnish evidence of its freedom from corrupt influences or influences opposed to basic democratic principles if there is reasonable cause to believe that —

(1) the organization has been suspended or expelled from, or is subject to other sanction, by a parent labor organization, or federation of organizations with which it had been affiliated, because it has demonstrated an unwillingness or inability to comply with governing requirements comparable in purpose to those required by subsection (a) of this section; or

(2) the organization is in fact subject to influences that would preclude recognition under this chapter.

(c) A labor organization which has or seeks recognition as a representative of employees under this chapter shall file financial and other reports with an Assistant Secretary of Labor for Labor Management Relations, provide for bonding of officials and employees of the organization, and comply with trusteeship and election standards.

(d) The Assistant Secretary shall prescribe such regulations as are necessary to carry out the purposes of this section. Such regulations shall conform generally to the principles applied to labor organizations in the private sector. Complaints of violations of this section shall be filed with the Assistant Secretary. In any matter arising under this section, the Assistant Secretary may require a labor organization to cease and desist from violations of this section and require it to take such action as he considers appropriate to carry out the policies of this section.

(e) This chapter does not authorize participation in the management of a labor organization or acting as a representative of a labor organization by a management official, a supervisor, or a confidential employee, except as specifically provided in this chapter, or by an employee if the participation or activity would result in a conflict or apparent conflict of interest or would otherwise be incompatible with law or with the official duties of the employee.

(f) In the case of any labor organization which by omission or commission has willfully and intentionally, with regard to any strike, work stoppage, or slowdown, violated section 7116(b)(7) of this title, the Authority shall, upon an appropriate finding by the Authority of such violation —

(1) revoke the exclusive recognition status of the labor organization, which shall then immediately cease to be legally entitled and obligated to represent employees in the unit; or

(2) take any other appropriate disciplinary action.

## SUBCHAPTER III — GRIEVANCES

### Sec. 7121. Grievance procedures

(a)(1) Except as provided in paragraph (2) of this subsection, any collective bargaining agreement shall provide procedures for the settlement of grievances, including questions of arbitrability. Except as provided in subsections (d) and (e) of this section the procedures shall be the exclusive procedures for resolving grievances which fall within its coverage.

(2) Any collective bargaining agreement may exclude any matter from the application of the grievance procedures which are provided for in the agreement.

(b) Any negotiated grievance procedure referred to in subsection (a) of this section shall —

(1) be fair and simple,

(2) provide for expeditious processing, and

(3) include procedures that —

(A) assure an exclusive representative the right, in its own behalf or on behalf of any employee in the unit represented by the exclusive representative, to present and process grievances;

(B) assure such an employee the right to present a grievance on the employee's own behalf, and assure the exclusive representative the right to be present during the grievance proceeding; and

(C) provide that any grievance not satisfactorily settled under the negotiated grievance procedure shall be subject to binding arbitration which may be invoked by either the exclusive representative or the agency.

(c) The preceding subsections of this section shall not apply with respect to any grievance concerning —

(1) any claimed violation of subchapter III of chapter 73 of this title (relating to prohibited political activities);

(2) retirement, life insurance, or health insurance;

(3) a suspension or removal under section 7532 of this title;

(4) any examination, certification, or appointment; or

(5) the classification of any position which does not result in the reduction in grade or pay of an employee.

(d) An aggrieved employee affected by a prohibited personnel practice under section 2302(b)(1) of this title which also falls under the coverage of the negotiated grievance procedure may raise the matter under a statutory procedure or the negotiated procedure, but not both. An employee shall be deemed to have exercised his option under this subsection to raise the matter under either a statutory procedure or the negotiated procedure at such time as the employee timely initiates an action under the applicable statutory procedure or timely files a grievance in writing, in accordance with the provisions of the parties' negotiated procedure, whichever event occurs first. Selection of the negotiated procedure in no manner prejudices the right of an aggrieved employee to request the Merit Systems Protection Board to review the final decision pursuant to section 7702 of this title in the case of any personnel action that could have been appealed to the Board, or, where applicable, to request the Equal Employment Opportunity Commission to review a final decision in any other matter involving a complaint of discrimination of the type prohibited by any law administered by the Equal Employment Opportunity Commission.

(e)(1) Matters covered under sections 4303 [performance appraisal systems] and 7512 [adverse actions] of this title which also fall within the coverage of the negotiated grievance procedure may, in the discretion of the aggrieved employee, be raised either under the appellate procedures of section 7701 of this title or under the negotiated grievance procedure, but not both. Similar matters which arise under other personnel systems applicable to employees covered by this chapter may, in the discretion of the aggrieved employee, be raised either under the appellate procedures, if any, applicable to those matters, or under the negotiated grievance procedure, but not both. An employee shall be deemed to have exercised his option under this subsection to raise a matter either under the applicable appellate procedures or under the negotiated grievance procedure at such time as the employee timely files a notice of appeal under the applicable appellate procedures or timely files a grievance in writing in accordance with the provisions of parties' negotiated grievance procedure, whichever event occurs first.

(2) In matters covered under sections 4303 and 7512 of this title which have been raised under the negotiated grievance procedure in accordance with this section, an arbitrator shall be governed by section 7701(c)(1) of this title, as applicable.

(f) In matters covered under sections 4303 and 7512 of this title which have been raised under the negotiated grievance procedure in accordance with this section, section 7702 of this title pertaining to judicial review shall apply to the award of an arbitrator in the same manner and under the same conditions as if the matter had been decided by the Board. In matters similar to those covered under sections 4303 and 7512 of this title which arise under other personnel systems and which an aggrieved employee has raised under the negotiated grievance procedure, judicial review of an arbitrator's award may be obtained in the same manner and on the same basis as could be obtained of a final decision in such matters raised under applicable appellate procedures.

### Sec. 7122. Exceptions to arbitral awards

(a) Either party to arbitration under this chapter may file with the Authority an exception to any arbitrator's award pursuant to the arbitration (other than an award relating to a matter described in section 7121(f) of this title). If upon review the Authority finds that the award is deficient —

(1) because it is contrary to any law, rule, or regulation;

(2) on other grounds similar to those applied by Federal courts in private sector labor-management relations;
the Authority may take such actions and make such recommendations concerning the award as it considers necessary, consistent with applicable laws, rules or regulations.

(b) If no exception to an arbitrator's award is filed under subsection (a) of this section during the 30-day period beginning on the date the award is served on the party, the award shall be final and binding. An agency shall take the actions required by an arbitrator's final award. The award may include the payment of backpay (as provided in section 5596 of this title).

### Sec. 7123. Judicial review; enforcement

(a) Any person aggrieved by any final order of the Authority other than an order under —

(1) section 7122 of this title (involving an award by an arbitrator), unless the order involves an unfair labor practice under section 7113 of this title, or

(2) section 7112 of this title (involving an appropriate unit determination),

may, during the 60-day period beginning on the date on which the order was issued, institute an action for judicial review of the Authority's order in the United States court of appeals in the circuit in which the person resides or transacts business or in the United States Court of Appeals for the District of Columbia.

(b) The Authority may petition any appropriate United States court of appeals for the enforcement of any order of the Authority and for appropriate temporary relief or restraining order.

(c) Upon the filing of a petition under subsection (a) of this section for judicial review or under subsection (b) of this section for enforcement, the Authority shall file in the court the record in the proceedings, as provided in section 2112 of title 28. Upon the filing of the petition, the court shall cause notice thereof to be served to the parties involved, and thereupon shall have jurisdiction of the proceeding and of the question determined therein and may grant any temporary relief (including a temporary restraining order) it considers just and proper and may make and enter a decree affirming and enforcing, modifying and enforcing as so modified, or setting aside in whole or in part the order of the Authority. The filing of a petition under subsection (a) or (b) of this section shall not operate as a stay of the Authority's order unless the court specifically orders the stay. Review of the Authority's order shall be on the record in accordance with section 706 of this title. No objection that has not been urged before the Authority, or its designee, shall be considered by the courts unless the failure or neglect to urge the objection is excused because of extraordinary circumstances. The findings of the Authority with respect to questions of fact, if supported by substantial evidence on the record considered as a whole, shall be conclusive. If any person applies to the court for leave to adduce additional evidence and shows to the satisfaction of the court that the additional evidence is material and that there were reasonable grounds for the failure to adduce the evidence in the hearing before the Authority, or its designee, the court may order the additional evidence to be taken before the Authority, or its designee, and to be made a part of the record. The Authority may modify its findings as to the facts, or make new findings by reason of additional evidence so taken and filed. The Authority shall file its modified or new findings, which, with respect to questions of fact, if supported by substantial evidence on the record considered as a whole, shall be conclusive. The Authority shall file its recommendations, if any, for the modification or setting aside of its original order. Upon the filing of the record with the court, the jurisdiction of the court shall be exclusive and its judgment and decree shall be final, except that the judgment and decree shall be subject to review by the Supreme Court of the United States upon writ of certiorari or certification as provided in section 1254 of title 23.

(d) The Authority may, upon issuance of a complaint as provided in section 7118 of this title charging that any person has engaged in or is engaging in an unfair labor practice, petition any United States district court within any district in which the unfair labor practice in question is alleged to have occurred or in which such person resides or transacts business for appropriate temporary relief or restraining order. Upon the filing of the petition, the court shall cause notice thereof to be served upon the person, and thereupon shall have jurisdiction to grant any temporary relief (including a temporary restraining order) it considers just and proper. A court shall not grant any temporary relief under this section if it would interfere with the ability of the agency to carry out its essential functions or if the Authority fails to establish probable cause that an unfair labor practice is being committed.

## SUBCHAPTER IV — ADMINISTRATIVE AND OTHER PROVISIONS

### Sec. 7131. Official time

(a) Any employee representing an exclusive representative in the negotiation of a collective bargaining agreement under this chapter shall be authorized official time for such purposes, including attendance at impasse proceeding, during the time the employee otherwise would be in a duty status. The number of employees for whom official time is authorized under this subsection shall not exceed the number of individuals designated as representing the agency for such purposes.

(b) Any activities performed by any employee relating to the internal business of a labor organization (including the solicitation of membership, elections of labor organization officials, and collection of dues) shall be performed during the time the employee is in a non-duty status.

(c) Except as provided in subsection (a) of this section, the Authority shall determine whether any employee participating for, or on behalf of, a labor organization in any phase of proceedings before the Authority shall be authorized official time for such purpose during the time the employee otherwise would be in a duty status.

(d) Except as provided in the preceding subsection of this section —

(1) any employee representing an exclusive representative, or

(2) in connection with any other matter covered by this chapter, any employee in an appropriate unit represented by an exclusive representative,

shall be granted official time in any amount the agency and the exclusive representative involved agree to be reasonable, necessary, and in the public interest.

## Sec. 7132. Subpenas

(a) Any member of the Authority, the General Counsel, or the Panel, any administrative law judge appointed by the Authority under section 3105 of this title, and any employee of the Authority designated by the Authority may —

(1) issue subpenas requiring the attendance and testimony of witnesses and the production of documentary or other evidence from any place in the United States; and

(2) administer oaths, take or order the taking of depositions, order responses to written interrogatories, examine witnesses, and receive evidence.

No subpena shall be issued under this section which requires the disclosure of intra-mangagement guidance, advice, counsel, or training within an agency and the Office of Personnel Management.

(b) In the case of contumacy or failure to obey a subpena issued under subsection (a)(1) of this section, the United States district court for the judicial district in which the person to whom the subpena is addressed resides or is served may issue an order requiring such person to appear at any designated place to testify or to produce documentary or other evidence. Any failure to obey the order of the court may be punished by the courts as a contempt thereof.

(c) Witnesses (whether appearing voluntarily or under subpena) shall be paid the same fee and mileage allowances which are paid subpenaed witnesses in the courts of the United States.

## Sec. 7133. Compilation and publication of data

(a) The Authority shall maintain a file of its proceedings and copies of all available agreements and arbitration decisions, and shall publish the texts of its decisions and the actions taken by the Panel under section 7119 of this title.

(b) All files maintained under subsection (a) of this section shall be open to inspection and reproduction in accordance with the provisions of sections 552 and 552a of this title.

## Sec. 7134. Regulations

The Authority, the General Counsel, the Federal Mediation and Conciliation Service, the Assistant Secretary of Labor for Labor Management Relations, and the Panel shall each prescribe rules and regulations to carry out the provisions of this chapter applicable to each of them, respectively. Provisions of subchapter II of chapter 5 of this title shall be applicable to the issuance, revision, or repeal of any such rule or regulation.

### Sec. 7135. Continuation of existing laws, recognitions, agreements, and procedures

(a) Nothing contained in this chapter shall preclude —

(1) the renewal or continuation of an exclusive recognition, certification of an exclusive representative, or a lawful agreement between an agency and an exclusive representative of its employees, which is entered into before the effective date of this chapter; or

(2) the renewal, continuation, or initial according of recognition for units of management officials or supervisors represented by labor organizations which historically or traditionally represent management officals or supervisors in private industry and which hold exclusive recognition for units of such officials or supervisors in any agency on the effective date of this chapter.

(b) Policies, regulations, and procedures established under and decisions issued under Executive Orders 11491, 11616, 11636, 11787, and 11838, or under any other Executive order, as in affect on the effective date of this chapter, shall remain in full force and effect until revised or revoked by the President, or unless superseded by specific provisions of the chapter or by regulations or decisions issued pursuant to this chapter.

†